ALONG CAME
A GARDENER

ALONG CAME
A GARDENER

DIANA STEVAN

ISLAND
HOUSE

ALONG CAME A GARDENER

Library and Archives Canada Cataloguing in Publication

ISBN 978-1-988180-25-0 (hardcover)

ISBN 978-1-988180-24-3 (ebook)

ISBN 978-1-988180-22-9 (paperback)

ISLAND
HOUSE

Cover design by Michael Stevantoni

Printed and bound in the United States

For my daughter Robyn,
who plants seeds of hope.

"This above all: to thine own self be true."

Hamlet

William Shakespeare

CONTENTS

The Seeds for This Book

Though I considered writing this book for decades, I only seriously began working on it during the COVID pandemic—a time that tested us all. This crisis robbed us of the social relationships that nurture us. Some of us weathered these challenges because of the support we had in our bubbles. Over Zoom calls and social media, we exchanged tales of hardships with friends and family. This became the standard way to stay in touch, linking the isolated with one another.

But many were truly alone, without the benefit of technology, which connected hundreds of millions around the globe. We watched television coverage of the elderly stuck behind glass in their care facilities, staring at their family members unable to visit them. Of the older adults we lost to COVID, I'm sure their sense of loneliness and abandonment were contributing factors in their deaths. Children and teens suffered, too, in immeasurable ways. Deprived of playtime and face-to-face communication with their peers, they lost precious years needed for social development. Whether you were old, young, or somewhere in between, the pandemic left its mark worldwide.

Where Would We Be Without Hope?

What kept many sane and reasonably content was hope—hope that the fears and daily reports of those struck down by COVID would soon stop. While many hoped and prayed the vaccine would help us return to the lives we once had, there were countless others who questioned its value. But regardless of our differences, hope got us through the pandemic. It helped us avoid depression by not giving in to the worldwide gloom. To manage, we had to accept what was happening and do what we could to raise our spirits, such as making video calls and sourdough. We ventured into nature, where it was safe to breathe the air even when we passed others on forest trails. We read books, watched films, listened to music, and took online courses to escape our misery and boredom. It all helped to counter the fear and loneliness brought on by the pandemic.

Though we can't see our worries, we know when we're hurting. When we're troubled, we don't sleep well. And then we're tired and cranky. We encounter physical problems when we don't exercise to keep our limbs supple and useful. Our self-esteem suffers when we indulge in junk food, especially when we're not hungry.

Overwhelmed, we can't see a solution. It's like standing at the base of a mountain shrouded in clouds; we can't see the top. But if we step forward and begin the climb, we can get there, one step at a time.

The work never stops for improving our lives. There's always something to do, some problem to solve. It's like a garden where weeds keep appearing year after year. If we ignore them, they multiply. Our lives can spiral out of control with too many negative thoughts weighing us down, keeping us rooted in one spot and stuck in our misery. That's when depression and anxiety hit the hardest. Hope—the sun on the horizon—can get us through.

Along Came a Gardener combines my love of gardening with what I learned during my twenty-five years as a family therapist.

When I first started practicing family therapy, I didn't realize how naïve I was. I believed I had all the answers. I had some, but I definitely had a lot to learn. As a therapist, I came across many stories—each unique, some heartbreaking, and many inspiring. But every one a gift. It was a blessing to meet with people from all walks of life. While helping many struggling with their problems, I also learned much to help myself, which is what I want to share with you.

And then there's my garden with its many lessons. Osamu Shimomura, one of three winners of the 2008 Nobel Prize in Chemistry, said, "Humans have learned various scientifically important matters, including genetics, by investigation of the various occurrences and mechanisms in nature; namely, we have learned from nature." I believe we also learn from Nature the art of good living.

I love seeing my garden wake up every spring like clockwork. The plants know when it's time to grow again, and such a miracle unfolds everywhere on the planet at different times of the year. Some plants, like the evergreens, seem to never sleep, remaining active and showing us their resilience. All we need to do is stop and consider what they're offering.

In this introduction, I'd like to leave you with one more note about Nature. S.R. Piccoli, in his book *Blessed Are the Contrar-*

ians: Diary of a Journey Through Interesting Times, writes that the great Galileo—the sixteenth-century Italian philosopher, astronomer, and mathematician considered to be the father of modern science—said in his homily for the feast of the Epiphany that God wrote the book of Nature in the language of mathematics. Galileo believed God gave humanity two books to guide them: the book of Sacred Scripture and the book of Nature. "And the language of nature is mathematics, so it is a language of God, a language of the Creator."

Galileo considered many paths to understanding our place in the universe. Not only did he study the stars and geometry, but he also explored art, poetry, and music. He famously said, "All truths are easy to understand once they are discovered; the point is to discover them."

And so, this is true when we look at our lives. We don't see all the possibilities. Occasionally, we need to pause and view them through a different lens. The fact you've picked up this book suggests you're interested in discovering what else is possible.

Names and circumstances have been altered in this book to protect people's privacy. I hope you find some inspiration within these pages.

The Landscape

LIFE AS A BED OF ROSES

How often have you heard that "life isn't a bed of roses"? It implies that life isn't all about beauty, love, and perfection. It isn't without struggle.

However, like life itself, a rose has thorns. A rose can represent both the beautiful and the painful parts of our journey.

No one goes through life unscathed. Every day newspapers publish articles and television stations broadcast news about people in trouble. They appear in the stories we read, watch on television or the big screen, and hear on podcasts or the radio. They could be wealthy or poor; isolated or a gang member; married or single; BIPOC or white; gay, straight, or any other sexual orientation; religious or not. Life doesn't discriminate. We all experience the trials of life. No human being escapes the emotional highs and lows.

In my practice, I talked to people from all walks of life. Every social class, colour, creed, and sexual orientation. The problems are similar. We're born, we embark on life's journey, we enjoy the good times, and we suffer the bad. Some of us get it worse than others. Some seem to have been born under a lucky star with more than their fair share of good fortune, while others seem to walk under a heavy cloud, encountering one catastrophe after another.

Each life's journey is unique. And yet, we all cry, laugh, brood, dream, complain, fear, love, and hope.

Life can go swimmingly along with nary a ripple until something goes wrong. Whether it's a blow from an unexpected illness, an accident, a death, a betrayal, a loss of fortune or any manner of bad luck. When we've been pricked by these thorns of misfortune, we can learn to cushion the blows. We can learn to soothe our wounds. We can learn how to make a hard path easier.

In other words, we can learn how to navigate around the thorns of our own making or through those that are unavoidable. We can grow in wisdom and manage the ones that come or avoid being hurt the same way in the future.

Roses Can Be Lethal

At first glance, the beauty of a rose's flower blinds us to what else is part of that plant. When we prick our finger on a rose, it may bleed or just hurt for a little while. But what if that thorn becomes embedded or the wound gets infected? What if that tiny cut grows into something that needs more than scant attention? What if it costs you your life?

The *Daily* Mail, a newspaper in the United Kingdom, reported such a story on March 20, 2010. George Emmerson, a seventy-three-year-old pensioner, was pruning a rose bush when he was pricked by a thorn. Unbeknownst to him, it became lodged in his finger, causing tremendous swelling. It appears he did little to deal with the infection, hoping it would go away in time. It didn't. He became seriously ill a week later and went to the hospital, where he was diagnosed with septicemia—blood poisoning. To treat it, the doctors cut off his finger and then amputated his arm to save his life. Unfortunately, the physical and mental trauma was too much to overcome. His heart gave out, and he died a week afterward, leaving behind a wife, three children, and three grandchildren.

This example illustrates how a small matter, if overlooked, can lead to a tragedy. This sad story reminds us of what's at stake when a hurt isn't tended to. What appeared to be a small matter turned out to be anything but. Though this is an example of an untended physical wound, how many lives have been wasted or lost because of untended emotional turmoil? Our feelings, whether big or small, show the extent to which we are coping. Like a barometer that indicates when the air pressure is high, the level of our emotions lets us know when we need to tend to them. The important thing is to pay attention to our feelings.

How many people despair and don't see any rainbow in their future? We need to tend to our hurts; we can't afford to let our wounds fester.

A SEED OF HOPE

I t's important to note that our capacity for growth is greater than we think. Neuroscientists have discovered that our brains keep growing and stabilize in early adulthood. Our brains continue to develop new neurons even in our eighties as long as we keep challenging ourselves intellectually and socially. Just as we learned in school that we can succeed if we apply ourselves, it is also true we can better our lives through self-examination, therapy, and other forms of knowledge. We all experience bumps in the road. Some seem insurmountable, but it's not always the case. That's when hope has a role to play.

Early in my counselling career, I worked for the Child Guidance Clinic in Winnipeg. As a clinical social worker (and later school psychologist), I visited schools and talked to classroom teachers, guidance counsellors, and special education instructors. School personnel referred children who were showing signs that all was not well in their lives. These were students who displayed aggressive tendencies or showed an inability to engage with others—which was especially worrisome if they were teens who could be at risk for suicide. Sometimes, that meant I would see the student alone in the guidance counsellor's office; other times, I'd arrange to meet with the student and their parents at their home or the clinic.

On one occasion, a high school guidance counsellor referred two sisters, who were gifted academically and artistically but failing miserably. One was an exceptional violinist; the other a talented poet who had attempted suicide. Their mother had been diagnosed with schizophrenia. Following the referral, I made a home visit to assess the family dynamics.

After meeting with the family, I had a better understanding of what the two sisters faced daily. Their father had a responsible executive position that took him away from home for long periods, leaving the three females of the household to work things out on their own. When the sisters came home from school, they never knew what mood they'd find their mother in. One minute, she was loving, and the next, she lashed out for little or no reason. Meanwhile, their father was of little help when he was home; he was a passive man, trying to hold on to his sanity. Given the mother's mental illness, family therapy was not practical.

Instead, I met with both sisters and listened while they poured out their problems. They complained about feeling rejected by their mother. They could do no right.

As we know, adolescence is a time for developing a sense of self and gaining more independence. However, adolescents still need their parents' support while they find their way.

The older sister kept expecting her mother to behave as she thought a mother should by showing love, warmth, and understanding. Given her mother's mental illness, her expectations were unrealistic. But who could blame her for wanting her mother's love? We all want our mother's love; we all need it.

It's not clear how much their mother loved them. She may have loved them dearly, but was unable to show it. She appeared stiff and remote, unable to engage. She could've been so preoccupied with her own existence that nothing else registered. Either way, the girls couldn't get the love they wanted. They kept trying to no avail. All they got for their efforts was an erosion of self, which added to their depression.

I empathized and reassured them that, given their mother's emotional challenges and erratic behaviour, it wasn't surprising they were having a hard time at school. In crisis, they couldn't see the personal resources they could draw on. We discussed strategies for dealing with someone unpredictable. Lowering expectations of their mother helped them step back and see how they could diffuse potentially volatile moments.

Rather than trying to change the people who are important to us, we need to look at *what we can do differently* about our situation. This way, we take responsibility for our own lives. We find the power within ourselves. The eldest sister did just that, and months later, wrote me the following poem. She gave me permission to share it with you.

The Seed of Hope

They had left me behind
but I did not mind,
for I was content
to live in darkness
and solitude.
No one there to hurt,
no one to start a feud,
no one there to rule me,
somewhere I could be free
I had all the comforts and food to survive;
yet I began to question why I was alive?
I began to shrivel up within and die,
when the gardener happened by.
Most would have thrown me to the wind, as he;
the prey of a ravenous chickadee.
But it was his wife, who reasoned
that it was just patience in need,
for the revival of life,
the emergence of seed.
No matter which direction
I tried to move
the walls of earth kept crumbling in;
it seemed impossible to win.
My world had become corrupt.

My only escape was up.
I hesitated below the surface,
fearing what lay ahead,
afraid I would not find a plow;
abandoned instead.
My determination was stronger than my fear
So I continued more excited
as I grew near.
As I broke through the earth
and met the sunlight,
my heart took to flight
for I'd found rebirth.
Though the tears of heaven
may splash against my face,
weeds try to win my place,
the wind whip and lash me
to the ground,
the sun wither my every leaf
I have faith, it is my belief.
That I can grow,
I have the resources to cope.
for I began below
from a simple seed of Hope.

There are many gardeners out there who are willing and able to plant these seeds of hope. From family members, friends, doctors, priests, ministers, rabbis, imams, counsellors, and psychiatrists to the neighbour next door.

But the seeds we plant in our garden can't do the work on their own. They need our help; they need nutrients, sun, water, and a decent environment. They need us to nurture the planted seed.

Besides finding empathic gardeners, we can also find the gardeners within when we work to improve our lives. Faith—in others, ourselves, and/or a higher power—can lead us on the path to recovery from the hurts we've experienced.

FAMILY LIFE, THEN AND NOW

Until the 1950s, many North American families followed a traditional model—a heterosexual union—with the father as the head of the family and the mother, for the most part, following his lead. They had clearly delineated roles: the father worked outside the home as the breadwinner, earning the household income. The mother stayed home, cooked, cleaned, and cared for the children. There were exceptions, but this was the norm. The double standard was also in place, ensuring women understood the value of being a virgin before marriage.

People were expected to weather any storms. To divorce was a no-no. The divorced were frowned upon, just as the unmarried were. Spinsters were pitied, as was the old bachelor. Childless marriages were suspect. As for the other sexual orientations, they may as well have been non-existent.

In many households, parents quickly put a stop to any behaviour considered inappropriate for the sex of their child. If their boys showed an interest in dolls or knitting, they would throw out or hide those objects regarded as strictly female toys or hobbies. Similarly, parents would admonish their girls for unladylike behaviour if they showed an interest in mechanics, used rough language, or dressed in masculine ways. Parents did so out of fear their children would be frowned upon and whispered about, making them pariahs in their communities.

I recall a girl in Grade 7 who wore loose clothes to hide the changes in her growing body. She had cut her hair in a boyish style and wore no makeup, even though her classmates had experimented with lipstick and rouge. Students whispered behind her back, saying she no longer liked boys. She was one of "them." We weren't aware of lesbian relationships then, but we recognized someone different from us. Same for boys who had a feminine gait or made gestures that looked affected coming from a male. If they didn't act boy-like, they were called queer, fruits, or homos—terms considered derogatory. Using the term gay to describe same-sex relationships was yet to come.

Back then, there seemed to be some kind of order, even with the days of the week. Sundays, stores were closed. Most people went to church. Though people practiced many faiths, it seemed the Christian faith dominated. Families followed the Ten Commandments, at least on the surface.

When anyone spoke about some infidelity, domestic abuse, or an unwanted pregnancy, it was whispered about behind closed doors. It was all hush-hush.

But around this time, cracks appeared in the traditional model. As the economy improved, and the youth became more and more educated, there seemed to be an awakening—a curiosity and questioning of what else life could offer. Books like *Peyton Place* and *Lady Chatterley's Lover* contained steamy sections of illicit sex.

These titillating pages, along with movies like *Some Like It Hot*, *The Seven Year Itch*, *Rebel Without a Cause*, *Splendor in the Grass,* and *The Apartment* exposed the underbelly, the craving many had for a less restrictive moral code.

Then, in the early years of the sixties, music, film, books, public demonstrations, and the drug culture promoted free love. Some couples tested that freedom by becoming swingers. They held parties where they exchanged partners for the night. Anthropologists, George and Nina O'Neill, caused a stir when they published *Open Marriage,* suggesting that as long as couples had good communication, they could have sex with others without breaking up.

With all these developments afoot, it's not surprising that families began to change. Young people questioned the church's teachings and the value of traditional family norms. Along with those questions came a greater openness to discuss sexuality. These changes were underlined by the arrival of the birth control pill. With the pill, women no longer had the fear of an unplanned pregnancy and being found out they were no longer virgins. They now had the same opportunity as men to experience sex before marriage. And when they learned about female orgasms, they were no longer happy leaving the bed without being satisfied themselves.

More Changes Were Coming

On June 28, 1969, the Stonewall riots—violent confrontations between homosexuals and the police outside a gay bar in New York City—inspired a new movement, the Gay Liberation Front.

Though strides were now being made, most people weren't ready to accept what had been hidden from view.

To many, homosexuality was still regarded as a mental illness. It wasn't until 1973—the year after I stopped working in a psychiatric ward—that homosexuality was removed from the *Diagnostic and Statistical Manual of Mental Disorders* (DSM). Around the same time, I worked with a psychologist who hid the fact he was gay. Though homosexuality was no longer regarded as an illness requiring treatment, the threat of stigma remained for those unwilling to risk coming out in their communities. Unable to live the life he wanted, he committed suicide. Distraught over what had happened to one of the nicest men I knew, I created a character loosely based on his life and wove him into my second novel, *The Rubber Fence*.

In Western cultures today, there is a growing awareness and understanding of the complexities of gender roles in our lives, especially for the young who are exploring their identity and place in the world. This has caused friction not only in families but in the public as a whole. In 2022, *The Guardian* newspaper reported that in the USA there were requests to ban 2,571 book titles—up thirty-eight per cent from 1,858 titles in 2021. Most of the books for which removal requests were made, said the American Library Association, were written by or about members of the LGBTQ+ community and people of colour.

Unfortunately, there are still many barriers to overcome depending on where you live, who you are, and what you believe. Many still grapple with what they think are *normal* expectations. I cringe when I hear about those who believe conversion therapy will convert someone who says they're gay to heterosexual, as if that were possible. Sadly, many people suffer because of rigid rules and ideas about their sexual orientation and their community's lack of understanding and compassion.

Nature dictates who we are. We can't change our sexual orientation no more than animals can change theirs. There are both heterosexual and homosexual animals, and other variations as well. Nature thrives on differences and variety. We can take a page from Nature's book.

Indigenous people have long recognized the non-binary people in their midst. The Canadian Museum for Human Rights website has a beautiful section on how Indigenous people practiced their sexuality before colonization. There are countless articles on their acceptance of all sexual variations. For example, gay people are seen by many Indigenous nations as two-spirit people—a gift to their communities. They often hold special positions. It seems the rest of the world is now playing catch-up.

The State of Marriage Today

People today don't settle down and form lifelong unions as quickly as generations past. They have more choices as to how they want to live out their adult years. Many opt to stay single rather than risk suffering through a loveless or conflict-ridden marriage like their parents. Those who are married will leave their partner when they don't get what they want from their union. Divorce is no longer a dirty word. But some partners leave without realizing they were part of the problem. Without that recognition, problems follow them into their next relationship.

Young people take longer to find "the one" and marry later in life than their parents' and grandparents' generations. Women have become increasingly educated and can provide for themselves. With greater gender equality and the erasure of the double standard, men and women no longer wait for marriage to have sexual relations. When they marry, they marry for love; they hope for mutual respect.

Men have also undergone a revolution, which has been troubling for many who are still grappling with what it means to be a man in today's world. In the last few decades, we've seen the growth of stay-at-home dads. While their wives work outside the home, they care for the children, make meals, and do the housework—duties formerly considered women's work. And in marriages where both spouses work, men are no longer expected to carry the entire financial burden of household expenses on their own. For many, the cost of living has become too high to support a family on only one salary.

I recently talked to a cousin who complained that her son hadn't worked for three years. When I asked her how her daughter-in-law, who is a teacher, felt about the arrangement, my cousin said, "She likes it. He makes the meals, does the washing, and takes the kids everywhere." I replied, "So, he's working hard." Her son's situation is an excellent example of role reversal, which is no longer unusual. Still, my cousin insisted on holding onto old thinking and old ways.

Today, the average age for marriage in the Western world is between twenty-seven and thirty. I got married at nineteen, right from my family home. My husband was twenty-four and hadn't lived on his own either. It was the early sixties, just before the sexual revolution arrived with threats to family unity. In retrospect, we now realize we were too young. Not too young to fall in love, but too young to understand our choice. Fortunately, we were able to ride the ups and downs of the rollercoaster of the sixties and its aftermath.

Taking your time to settle down has its benefits. Many prefer a marriage-like union to test the waters or just because they no longer consider the institution of marriage beneficial. As a result, the divorce rate has come down. But women who are waiting longer to get married may find they're waiting too long to have children. They have less time than men to procreate without risk of complications. Couples wait because they fear they won't be able to focus on their career, worry they can't afford to raise kids, and stress about the future. Because of these fears, more and more people are choosing not to have children.

Polyamory

And then, there's polyamory. It's defined as "a relationship structure in which three or more adults form a long-term, committed relationship," according to *Maclean's* September 2024 story "Whole Lotta Love" by writer Rosemary Counter. She describes variations that harken back to the 1970s when swinging and open marriages were both contemplated and practiced. I can't imagine the challenges for all parties involved in any form of polyamory today. As a therapist, my experience was with couples, either gay or straight, who struggled with the complexities of being in a committed relationship with someone from a different background. But people always search for the ideal, even if it means straying from the norm. I would have had difficulty sorting out any conflicts that might arise in these complicated polyamorous relationships.

Child-Rearing

Child-rearing has also evolved. Not long ago—a few generations back—a child was seen but not heard. Their voice didn't matter or count like it does today. We now know the harm done in families where the rod or strap was used. We frown on spanking and show more respect for the child. Some would argue children have too much power today. There was a time when teachers could count on the child's parents for support when there were discipline problems at school. This is no longer the case. Hopefully, the pendulum will swing back so we can find a happy balance—one where teachers and parents work together to support the child's intellectual, social, and emotional growth.

Family Life Today

So, what makes up a family today? We have extended families with three to four generations living under one roof, mixed marriages, gay couples with children, single-parent families, blended families, and more. Each one is valid.

With travel made easy, families can move around not only for adventure but also for work opportunities. As a result, families are stretched and fragmented around the world. Regardless of the physical distance between family members today, what occurs in our families, in childhood, and later in life continues to affect us. What happens at home is imprinted on our memories. How we were treated by those we love stays with us throughout life. The good times and the bad.

But it seems many of us remember the hurts more often than the joys. They never leave us. Depending on the severity and amount, our wounds can haunt us if we let them. It's helpful to be aware of them, as they can trigger us at unexpected times. Trauma of any kind can linger if not dealt with.

Neglected Garden, Neglected Life

I take a second look whenever I pass a house with a lawn full of weeds and the odd bit of junk. A choke-filled mess covers the whole yard, where flowers find little room to bloom or the nutrients to survive. A weed-choked landscape is a blemish on the beauty of the neighbourhood. It threatens the lands nearby by allowing the seeds of the weeds to spread to well-tended gardens. However, because of concerns about pesticides and other chemicals that affect the insects and birds that visit our gardens, there has been a trend to 'wild' the garden and let it fill with native flowers and other plants. Wilding is not the same as neglect; it's a way of managing the landscape in harmony with nature; the one that incorporates debris isn't.

The same can be said of the neglected life that isn't nurtured. It affects family, friends, and anyone around them. Indeed, life is not without struggle. There are countless ways to give up on yourself, but there are also countless ways to take on life's challenges. How many stories have you read about people who've lived through harsh circumstances yet found the will to keep going and persevere against all odds? Nelson Mandela, an anti-apartheid activist, spent twenty-seven years in prison but never gave up hope. When he was finally released, he continued his fight to end apartheid and became the first president of South Africa. Terry Fox, a Canadian athlete who lost a leg to cancer, found the will to keep going and ran across Canada to raise money for cancer research. His spirit and determination have inspired millions to keep going when life gets rough.

But then there are those who falter. They're not as strong, but not less worthy. They're the ones who need the support of family, friends, or professionals. And though help is available, they stay in the shadows, giving into despair, their spirits crushed. They've forgotten the strength they once had. They've forgotten how to ask for help or have given up trying.

Right from the time we are born, we seek help. We cry when we're cold and wet, hungry, or miserable. We learn that when we raise our voices, help will come. And as the months go by, we try to sit up by ourselves, then crawl. We want to move on our own and explore our environment. Even as babies, we are already headed for the road to independence. We try to walk, taking our first steps when we are between nine and fourteen months old.

Anyone who has a child or has been around infants taking their first steps knows how they struggle to keep going. They may rely on a human hand to help them. If a hand isn't available, they'll try to get up by holding on to the seat of a chair or a table leg. They venture forward on wobbly legs, only to fall. Do they stay down? Do they say, 'Well, that didn't work,' and return to crawling? No, they get up and try again and again. Nothing stops infants from walking, no matter how many times they've fallen. They keep at it, as if to say: "Where there's a will, there's a way."

And yet, many adults give up. They walk with their heads bent and their shoulders stooped. We don't know what troubles they're carrying. We don't know what's weighing them down, but we recognize they've reached a point where they feel they have no options.

In Vancouver, the homeless gather in a poor area on Hastings and Main Street. I lived in the city for a long time and witnessed people from all walks of life suffering from mental health and addiction problems—the educated and the illiterate, the once rich and the poor, the able-bodied and the weak. They shuffle up and down the streets looking for their next fix or companionship, some with shopping carts full of meagre possessions.

When people reach this point, the weeds of despair take over. There are few or none they can trust to hold them up. Perhaps their support system gave up when the addict and the mentally ill individual gave up. Since each human being walking the streets is unique, who is to judge or condemn their behaviour? We don't know their lives; we don't know the misfortunes that brought them to this point. We don't know their story, but we know they're hurting. Home is now in a public place because they can't afford any other option. They sleep in tents in city parks, along sidewalks, or wherever they can find a spot of land to lay their heads.

Their obvious plight—doing drugs openly on the streets, screaming obscenities in public spaces, sleeping in shop doorways—disturbs people who take pride in their community. When tourists pass this troubled area in Vancouver, they are shocked to witness this human tragedy. Municipal officials view these streets peopled with the poor as blights in the city. Families complain of needles and excrement in parks where tents for the homeless have taken over. No matter which group you're a member of, it's a sad situation.

Many of these poor souls have been dealt a bad hand. We now know genetics plays a big part in mental illness and drug addiction. Coupled with a challenging childhood, significant losses, and poverty, it's hard to find a way out. Thankfully, many people are working hard to help the needy. They are providing everything from supervised injection sites to adequate housing and counselling support to give them a leg up.

My work involved helping individuals who hadn't yet reached that point when all hope was lost. Their plight wasn't visible on the street. They wanted help with depression and other emotional problems; they had difficulty getting out of bed to go to work or being there for their children. The weeds they'd neglected in their lives had shown up as conflict in their relationships at home, in their workplace, or in their community. Or all three. They'd suffered an unexpected blow—a divorce, a job loss, an accident, the death of someone they loved, or some other traumatic event—and were lashing out, retreating to the safety of their minds, or numbing their feelings with drugs.

The Unexpected

Not surprisingly, the unexpected can throw us for a loop. Any traumatic event can lead to desolation and become the neglected garden, the neglected life.

Nature has similar challenges. Winter storms with heavy snow and ice can bend and break branches, killing otherwise healthy vegetation. Heavy rain in the spring or summer can wash away soil and seed. With its accompanying hordes of insects, drought can damage a plant to the point of no return. A proliferation of weeds can choke out the most beautiful plants if allowed to multiply.

For humans, it's divorce, loss of a loved one, sickness, addiction, mental illness, job loss, housing insecurity, bankruptcy, poverty, accidents, family conflict, and toxic relationships and work environments. As with Nature, the list is endless.

How do we weather unexpected storms in life?

Many rely on their faith to give them strength. Others lean on friends and loved ones. Some on learned resilience. We can also do it by taking care of ourselves, ensuring we are in the best health—physically, mentally, and spiritually.

Taking Care of Those First Weeds

Most of us get through our days with only a few weeds bugging us. But sometimes, even just one can be especially bothersome and stubborn to remove.

Overlooked or buried, an angry word or a slight from someone we love or encounter can fester. Like a nuisance weed, it must be dealt with sooner than later to prevent it from multiplying and becoming an unmanageable problem.

There are many reasons people give up. They may have tried in the past, but nothing helped to improve their lot. And yet, as mentioned, we've all heard about people who've survived unimaginable tragedies and continued on, eventually finding love and laughter. My grandmother (baba) and mother, whom I wrote about in *Lukia's Family Saga,* my historical fiction series, come to mind. My baba, Lukia Mazurec, lost four of her children, her husband, and her home during WWI, and survived life in a refugee camp, the Bolshevik Revolution, a typhus epidemic, a civil war, and the Polish occupation. At age fifty-five, she brought her remaining children to Canada just before the Great Depression began. When she was sixty-nine, she moved into my parents' home to help take care of me. Despite what she had endured, she found joy in her life. What I remember is a contented woman who would laugh and sing folk songs around the dining table after supper.

There are countless stories of people who survived the Holocaust when all their relatives had perished. They somehow carried on. But not without pain. I'm sure there were many moments when they recalled what they'd gone through but figured out how to live again.

How did they do it? How did they find hope on the horizon when the clouds seemed too much to bear? How did they find the rainbow after the rain?

I know for my baba, it was grit, determination, and faith that kept her going. She relied on her Orthodox church. She got down on her knees and prayed daily, often more than once. Though she grieved her losses, she put her energy into caring for her remaining children. And she kept busy. "So busy," my cousin said, "she had no time for tears."

Thankfully, there are ways to head off those grey days. There are ways to keep our faith and spirits up, even during the trying times we've been living in. It means taking small steps with one foot in front of the other, even if it means risking a fall again. Like working in a garden, dealing with life's challenges takes hard work and determination.

You just need to remember you were a baby once, and when you began to walk, you didn't give up even though you kept falling. As the Japanese say, fall down seven times, stand up eight.

When Problems Pile Up

Looking around your circle of friends, family, and colleagues, you might not find the support you need to figure out how to move forward. Perhaps the ones close to you are part of the problem. If, after every encounter, you walk away with an uneasy feeling—that you don't count, that you're not measuring up, that you're to blame—you may need to seek support outside your circle.

That's when going to a therapist becomes a wise choice. And thankfully, today, going to a therapist is a socially sanctioned choice as well. Many enlightened employers provide confidential employee and family counselling services as one of their benefits.

A therapist understands and accepts that life challenges are often difficult to deal with on your own. With a professional—therapist, psychiatrist, clinical social worker, psychologist, or clinical counsellor—you can talk freely about what's troubling you and gain some perspective. Not invested in your situation, a therapist sees possibilities for change that you don't. And through their guidance, you can begin to view your situation through a different lens. The therapist is bound by their professional bodies to provide a safe environment where you can speak in confidence about whatever is on your mind.

Seeing a therapist is like playing an open game of cards. In a hand held close to your chest, it's hard to tell what's what. But if you lay your cards on the table, you can see what you have to play with. You gain some emotional distance. Pouring out your problems can help you see what's keeping you churning in the same spot.

I suspect some of you might say, 'But I'm not the one who's the problem. Why should I go for help?' Fair enough. But if a significant other person in your life doesn't think they have a problem and is unwilling to seek therapy or counselling, you do have a problem and can at least get some comfort and emotional distance yourself. Only then can you look more critically at what can be done to change the dynamic that troubles you. And you may even discover that you've contributed to the problem by unwittingly reinforcing unhealthy behaviour. Or you may need help to walk away.

Sometimes our expectations are unrealistic, and that alone can mess us up. We need to manage them as well. Hope is critical, but we also need to be realistic.

A single mother was having trouble with her rebellious twenty-year-old daughter. It seemed no matter what she did, she was met with verbal abuse. Their living situation had become intolerable and yet the mother found it hard to be assertive without being abusive herself. When her daughter refused to go with her for family counselling, the mother decided to go on her own. With the help of a therapist, she learned how to confront her daughter without resorting to tit-for-tat behaviour. She also laid out some ground rules for her daughter if she wanted to continue living at home.

Sometimes, we cling to our old ways because we're afraid to let go and consider a new way of being, a new way of thinking. We get comfortable in the predictability of our lives, even if we are suffering in our weed-filled garden.

Like the gardener who ignored the thorn from the rose, leaving emotional pain to build up with no examination is asking for trouble. That kind of pain can become so unbearable that sufferers end up physically hurting themselves or others. They might land in a psychiatric ward or some bar, trying to drown their sorrows, or seek solace through affairs or drugs. They might also leave a marriage and their children—a union once built on love—without looking inward and exploring their options.

Without some introspection and willingness to reflect on our hurt and try something different, we are destined to repeat unhealthy patterns, even with new partners in life. Just as we need a mirror to see our physical self, we need others to help us see our emotional self. And that's where psychotherapists—the emotional gardeners—come in.

Asking for Help

It takes courage to ask for help. It's admitting we don't have all the answers and can't fix our problems alone. Seeking help from a therapist is a relatively recent phenomenon. For the masses, that kind of support only found favour in the late twentieth century.

But everyone who makes that call for help is on their way to solving their problems. They hope life can improve and are willing to share their issues with a professional. They're showing they are eager to open themselves up to scrutiny and learn new ways of thinking and being. Not an easy thing to do.

I know firsthand how agonizing it can be to ask for help. My husband and I are both social workers. We wrongly assumed we could work out our issues because of our training. *Wrong.* Like those we treated, we couldn't think straight when we were emotionally upset. We blurted out things we later regretted. Eventually, we took that big step and went for marital therapy, together and alone. We've since gone for help with other concerns, like unresolved grief, family conflict, and workplace bullying.

In my therapy practice, I often said to those considering separation or divorce, "I understand the trauma you're going through. Though I've been married for decades, there were times my husband and I considered leaving the relationship. We are thankful we didn't, but we know the pain of conflict when nothing you say or do seems to change the course. We understand how assigning and taking blame feels. But we've also experienced the bliss that comes from working through our difficulties. We didn't physically split, but we weren't always there for each other emotionally like we needed to be."

Again, giving ourselves permission to see a therapist was one of the best things we did to save our marriage.

It's important to remember that we cannot control the behaviour of others. The only person we have control over is ourselves. If we change how we respond, then the one we're in conflict with is also likely to change. It's one way to eliminate the weeds choking our life's garden and find some room for flowers to brighten our day.

THE GARDENERS

A Green Thumb

My grandmother and mother, who were farmers in Ukraine and Canada, passed on their love of gardening to me. My mother had a lush garden covering half a city lot in Winnipeg. Though her life on the farm was long over, her understanding of plants and how to amend soil served her well. She grew potatoes, onions, garlic, corn, cucumbers, tomatoes, green and yellow beans, peas, carrots, cabbage, beets, dill, and rhubarb. She grew so much that she shared the abundance with her neighbours and the roomers who lived upstairs in our home. She shared her love of food—freshly picked. I don't remember her using any chemical fertilizers. Everything was organic, from the manure she got from a local farm to the love she gave every plant. She and my baba would be out daily, hoeing the weeds, thinning and watering the plants, and harvesting the fruits of their labour. If Mom wasn't outside working in her garden, she was often inside canning or freezing fruits and vegetables for the winter.

Though I have a green thumb, I still consult friends, books, and workers in the garden centres where I buy our plants. They have the knowledge and expertise I can count on when tackling an insect problem, figuring out where to put a specific plant, or deciding what would work best in an area that needs filling.

The Garden of Our Minds

The garden of our minds is not that different. We can't always figure things out alone, especially when feeling emotional. Emotions cloud our judgment and our ability to see the entire problem. That's when therapists can help. There is no longer a stigma around having one. The only stigma that may remain is in our own heads and hearts, which doesn't serve us when we are in trouble.

No Man Is an Island

When English poet John Donne wrote in *Meditation XVII* that "no man is an island," he spoke about the interconnectedness of us all. He asked us to consider what we offer to one another and take up that offer. We don't have to suffer alone.

Similarly, no tree is an island. In his bestseller *Hidden Life of Trees,* author Peter Wohlleben writes about how trees share water and nutrients, suggesting that they use their "maternal instincts" to nurture the weaker ones in their surroundings. The oldest trees are resources for the youngest; those nearing death give up much of their carbon to younger neighbouring trees. And if a tree finds an insect intent on devouring its leaves and bark, it sends an alarm signal to others in their community. Trees not only rely on one another to survive, but they also rely on other life forms.

Trees and fungi have a special bond. They form partnerships known as mycorrhiza. The thread-like fungi wrap themselves around the roots of a tree, helping it get water and nutrients like phosphorus and nitrogen. In exchange, the tree makes carbon-rich sugars for the fungi through photosynthesis. Talk about good neighbours!

A Brief History of Psychotherapy

It's worth taking a look at how psychotherapy became accepted by the public, if only to ease our minds that we're now living in an age when going to a therapist is a wise choice for many. It all started with Freud in the 1890s and developed from there. He used hypnosis and free association to analyze dreams and the psychological woes of his patients. It was an effective treatment for neuroses, but it took time. Years and money!

Later, psychotherapy was depicted in literature and movies as a practice mainly reserved for the rich. Films in 1950s and 1960s New York showed characters visiting their psychiatrist often—sometimes weekly—to lie on their couch in lavish offices and unload their troubles. Meanwhile, the psychiatrist took notes, nodded, and occasionally uttered something that spurred their patients to dig deeper into their early childhood.

Woody Allen used regular sessions with his psychoanalyst in his screenplays. In psychoanalysis, the therapist says little during the hour-long sessions but encourages the patient to blurt out what's on their mind. There are leading questions, and the patient's mother is a prime focus. The hope is the patient will find their way out of a morass by revealing repressed childhood memories—the ones that leave scars.

With the discovery of psychotropic drugs in the late 1940s, 1950s, and 1960s, psychoanalysis fell out of favour. As well, psychiatrists, psychologists, and social workers developed new psychotherapeutic approaches that showed results in a shorter time, and therefore were more cost-effective. We learned that psychoanalysis is only one way to begin healing any emotional wounds. As well, this type of therapeutic approach doesn't answer all the questions. Mother isn't the only one responsible for all that goes wrong. In some psychiatric circles, she was often unfairly blamed, as if the father had no role to play at all. Was he absent? Was he silent? Was he encouraging his wife from the sidelines or was he colluding with the child, pitting them against his spouse to deal with his own issues? There are so many ways a parent can influence a child's behaviour. Looking at the entire family system, with its particular communication patterns, is another way of finding answers. Besides the mother, there's a father, siblings, other assorted relatives, influential figures in our environment, and genetics—our nature. They all contribute to who we are and how we cope.

The Idea of Psychotherapy Blossomed

With self-help books published in the 1960s, like *I'm OK-You're OK* and *Games People Play*, the general population began looking inward. This movement exploded in the 1970s, the period author Tom Wolfe first identified in an essay entitled "The 'Me' Decade and the Third Great Awakening." Suddenly, it seemed more and more people were taking the time to examine their lives. Some dismissed it as navel-gazing, but many were awakened by new possibilities. They began to think they weren't necessarily stuck in some family script they hadn't written. They could take control. Some even looked to the stars for clues about their personalities. The field of astrology and the cult of numerology gained followers.

Until the 1970s, the general population expected to solve psychological and social problems independently, even when their emotions ran high. To admit you couldn't manage was a mark against you. The idea of seeing someone outside your immediate family or intimate circle of friends for emotional help was a novelty. Many felt disloyal or embarrassed to reveal intimate secrets, even if they weighed them down in despair. Still, counselling and therapy gained popularity in the eighties and nineties. Seeing a professional for help with personal issues became acceptable, even though it was still hard to admit you couldn't solve problems alone.

Employee assistance programs (EAPs) and employee and family assistance programs (EFAPs) were now being offered as benefits in various workplaces. During this time, I worked as a counsellor (and later the director) at Interlock in Burnaby, British Columbia. This non-profit agency arranged confidential employee counselling benefits for different occupational groups. We assisted lawyers, chartered accountants, bank employees, teamster union members, mariners, teachers, and janitors. Occasionally, I had to reassure clients who had phoned they were doing the right thing by asking for help. They'd taken the first step to solving their problems by admitting they needed outside help and finding the courage to make an appointment.

When I used to visit various workplaces to promote this benefit, I would say, "We go quickly to our family doctor for any ailment, the dentist if a tooth keeps us awake at night, the vet with our sick pet, and the mechanic when our car breaks down, and yet, for matters of the mind, we think we should be able to figure it out ourselves. Why would we think that when the brain is the most unexplored part of our bodies? Scientists are still trying to figure out how our brains work."

The Evolution of Family Therapy

Around the time Freud began listening to his patients in hopes of understanding how the mind works, private charities were sending workers to the homes of the poor to see how they were managing as a whole. These social services were concerned about home stability, adequate shelter, and food. None of what these workers did was considered family therapy; they called it a family and home assessment. But their work certainly raised the value of seeing a whole family in their home to discover what care and comforts of life its members were getting. It helped social services understand how home life was affecting well-being.

It wasn't until the 1970s that the idea of family therapy began to flourish among other mental health professionals. Suddenly, whole families were being seen, recorded, and discussed at various academic institutions training social workers, psychologists, and psychiatrists at work in mental health settings. Therapists could see firsthand what their patients were complaining about.

These family therapists focused on the kind of nurture and messages we get from our family, as shown through their words and actions. Even if the trained family therapist saw an individual client seeking help, it was helpful to have knowledge of the family system and how it positively or negatively affected their mental health.

An unloving home environment hampers the psychosocial development of children and also affects those in charge. A myriad of personal problems can be traced to family systems with unhealthy communication. Though I'm sure these original family therapists accepted the power of genetics, their primary focus was the family environment. They could do little about what we come into the world with, but they hoped to make a difference through therapy.

The notable therapists at the time were American. Jay Haley and Salvador Minuchin were from Philadelphia; Virginia Satir, Gregory Bateson (married to anthropologist Margaret Mead), and Don D. Jackson practiced out of Palo Alto, California. They had all moved beyond Freud and were no longer focusing primarily on the mother, the one the psychoanalyst had determined was responsible for shaping the child's behaviour. Instead of solely blaming the mother, they were now looking at the whole family and its dynamics. These therapists were studying all aspects of family and marital communication, both verbal and non-verbal. They assessed not only what family members say to one another but also how they respond—or don't respond—through their facial expressions, tone, and body language.

These family therapists travelled the globe spouting their theories. I attended international conferences in Philadelphia and New York, where renowned therapists explained the benefits of seeing the whole family. They spoke of the power contained in the family unit—the power to encourage or discourage those within.

Virginia Satir, Jay Haley, and R.D. Laing came to Winnipeg to show new family therapists how to help families solve their problems. They illustrated how family members influenced one another and either helped or hindered their progress in life. As therapists ourselves, we went through exercises showing how body language affected those close to us. We learned how to interpret these signs in our work with families.

Becoming a Therapist

In my master's program in the early 1970s, I was fortunate to have social worker Dr. Gerald Erickson as my mentor during my training. He had spent ten years as a family therapist at a Wisconsin mental health centre before accepting a position as a professor in the School of Social Work at the University of Manitoba.

Because of his influence, I specialized in family therapy and read all the literature available about this relatively new approach. Gurus in the field were basically saying that the family system affected the behaviour of its members, even causing mental illness. The practice of family therapy was new and hot then. It helped shine a spotlight on how we communicate in our families, deal with conflict, show affection, and let one another know what we need.

It was an exciting time to be a therapist. As a student and later as a therapist in a psychiatric ward and at a child guidance clinic, colleagues and I videotaped sessions with families who came to us for help. Afterwards, we would gather with fellow therapists to interpret what we saw and decide how to help the family make a positive shift in their communication practices. We also observed one another's work through a one-way mirror and reviewed these sessions with other social workers, psychologists, and psychiatrists.

The psychotherapy gurus seemed to say it didn't matter what nature you came into the world with; what was important was the nurturing you got. We went from blaming everything wrong on nature to blaming everything on nurture. In the following decades, we learned that was also a mistake. Today, experts in the field are stressing nature more than nurture in our development. Nurture is flexible. Nature is set. We cannot help the cards we've been dealt. What we can do, however, is choose how we play with them and what cards we will favour.

I not only analyzed the communication patterns of couples and families I saw in counselling, but I also examined my family of origin and then the nuclear one I had with my husband and our two daughters. Though I was a therapist, it didn't mean I had the solutions to all the problems that came up with my family. It's the classic dilemma. How many have heard that the cobbler's children go barefoot? When those proficient in certain practices strive for excellence, they can easily overlook the needs of those in their immediate environment. It's difficult to see your own issues. It's hard to step outside yourself and see how you can be at fault and how you need to change.

Therapists are often people seeking answers themselves as to how they can make things better. They are usually highly compassionate beings, aware of others' pain. They wish to not only understand but to help. And even though they are trained to help others with their emotional distress, they too can't see clearly when their emotions are heightened. Even therapists see other therapists when they get stuck.

Working in Mental Health

Upon graduating with a Master of Social Work in 1972, I began work as a social worker in a psychiatric ward at the Winnipeg General Hospital (now known as the Health Sciences Centre). Trained as a family therapist, I worked as a co-therapist with psychiatric interns who were learning how to work with their patients' families. We interviewed these families in the ward and their homes.

The ward's mentally ill included individuals who had become depressed over some life event and those who heard voices and saw things that weren't there. There were also patients who swung from a dark mood to euphoria and back again.

Each person who suffers from mental illness is unique and can't be pigeonholed. They're often hard to diagnose. I've seen patient charts that had one diagnosis at the beginning of their treatment and another weeks later. We know how difficult it can be to diagnose a physical ailment. Mental suffering is even harder to analyze.

In short-stay units—like the one I was assigned to—psychiatrists have little time to look for the underlying causes. There's pressure to get patients out quickly as hospital beds are at a premium and the demand is high. Most people who end up in a psychiatric ward have been storing their emotional pain for years, sometimes decades. The life events or circumstances that led to their hospital admission must be unravelled and understood. So, expecting them to get their lives together in a short-stay ward is a tall order for both patients and staff. The whole situation is fraught with false hope. The most you can hope for is a good patch job.

Psychiatrists arrive at a diagnosis by reviewing patient histories, their behaviour on admission, and what family and friends might contribute. They refer to a handbook called the *Diagnostic and Statistical Manual of Mental Disorders* (DSM), which gives a series of symptoms for each diagnosis. From time to time, the American Psychiatric Association revises and updates its diagnostic criteria for the various categories of mental disorders. The practice of psychiatry is not an exact science, but it's one we rely on to help the mentally ill.

Patients are often treated with psychotherapy, drugs, and/or electric shock treatment—yes, it's still happening today, in some places more than ever—and then sent home with plans for follow-up by a mental health professional in the community. Treatment also entails determining who is hindering the mentally ill person's treatment and either working with them to get them on their side or discouraging the patient from seeing them again. It's also imperative to marshal social resources—often through the social worker—so that the patient has a greater chance of survival once they're back in the community. Once they are discharged, they will need support and understanding from the pertinent people in their lives—friends, family, employers, or coworkers. They will need help to muster up their inner resources as they begin their road to recovery. What is truly sad is the fact that there is a lack of services and not enough time to hear the stories that led a patient down a dark rabbit hole.

In my early years of working in mental health, I was against drugs. I thought understanding and love paved the way to better health. I wasn't entirely wrong, but I was naïve. Some mentally ill patients need more than that to recover. Along with psychotherapy, they will require drugs to deal with their mental health conditions.

The introduction of new psychotropic medication—first prescribed in 1950—put a stop to many barbaric psychiatric practices that were used in the past, like lobotomies, insulin coma therapy, chemically induced seizures, straitjackets, and hydrotherapy. Medication lifts the spirits of the depressed and hopefully motivates them to work on their problems through psychotherapy. Those diagnosed with a bipolar condition need it to even out their moods. Those who have hallucinations and hear voices need medication so they can live a more normal life.

Drugs also help to calm some elderly patients with dementia who act aggressively toward caregivers in their speech and behaviour. There are countless stories of adult children who have suffered through a personal attack from a parent—once loving and now angry—because of a personality change brought on by the onset of Alzheimer's. Given the right drug, the afflicted can lead a more contented life. As can their caregivers.

Today, there are no longer insane asylums as they were called back then. In the late 1960s and 1970s, the public became aware of the primitive mental health practices used to control the mentally ill. The novel *One Flew Over the Cuckoo's Nest*, which was adapted into a movie, fuelled public outrage. Lawyers got involved and demanded patient rights, which were sorely needed. Too many people were being admitted and held involuntarily. But in hindsight, the authorities who closed down these mental health institutions threw the baby out with the bath water. Now, those who could benefit—from a place that administers drugs when needed and provides shelter, food, and protection from those who might take advantage—roam our streets talking to themselves or the people they see in their hallucinations.

A Variety of Work Settings

I was fortunate to have worked as a psychotherapist in various clinical settings—a psychiatric ward, a community mental health centre, a child guidance clinic, a residential treatment centre for children, a cancer care clinic, an employee and family assistance counselling agency, and my private practice. Treating people of all ages from all walks of life taught me much about human behaviour.

The longer I worked as a psychotherapist, the more I believed that much of the answers to life's problems lie within each of us. When our minds are clouded with emotion, our inability to see, hear, and think clearly prevents us from solving issues independently. Who can think with an open mind when they're upset? Have you ever tried to reason with someone who is yelling at you? Or sobbing out of control? Or withdrawing and refusing to communicate? They are so caught up in their own pain that nothing can get through. They can only reflect on what's happened when they've had a chance to cool off and settle down. But then again, we are all unique. One size doesn't fit all. Their pile of hurt may be so heavy they believe their only way out is to hurt themselves or others.

When I worked for an employee and family counselling services agency, the people who came to see me accepted they had a problem they couldn't solve on their own. Counselling gave them an opportunity to reveal their problems in confidence and see them with fresh eyes. Because they were motivated and accepted the need for change, I felt more like a guide, showing them what they might be missing on an unknown trail. Sometimes, it meant facing the obvious, confronting reality—seeing the elephant in the room and not being afraid to say there's an elephant in the room, which is often the case in families that have members with addiction and personality disorders.

Sometimes, no matter what we do, the problems in our relationships won't be resolved until the one suffering admits they have a problem and gets help themselves. But they need to want to change. The adage that "you can lead a horse to water but you can't make him drink" is worth remembering. It relates well to the efficacy of counselling.

Seeking Help

Though it's become easier to seek help, services vary from place to place. In some countries, like Canada and the United Kingdom, there's universal health care, which means psychiatric services are covered if your family doctor refers you. You can also seek free help through a government-run mental health centre or access community programs that offer counselling on a sliding scale. Besides public offerings, you can also see a private practitioner—a social worker or psychologist—who charges by the hour.

And, since many workplaces globally offer free, confidential employee and family assistance programs (EFAPs), you can check your workplace to see if this benefit is available. If your employer does not offer it, you could mention its value to management. Adding an EFAP to an employee's benefit package is relatively inexpensive. Employers worldwide have found that employees are more productive and happier when they get help to deal with stress on and off the job.

However, an EFAP is a short-term counselling practice; typically, it offers anywhere from three to seven sessions, depending on the provider. Many seeking help will get what they need within that period. It starts them on the path to improve their life. Those who need more sessions to recover from their years of pain are referred to other therapists for longer-term therapy. Though some may not be able to afford the long game, it's better to get some counselling than none at all. And with some EFAPs, the client can have their allotted number of sessions, then wait a short period before contacting the agency again for another round of counselling with the same therapist.

THE SOIL

NATURE, THE INSTRUCTOR

The debate on the causes of concerning behaviour continues today—how much are we affected by nature and how much by nurture? This age-old argument shows no sign of letting up.

Anyone who has children knows each infant arrives with their own personality. This isn't unique to humans. Pet lovers recognize differences in temperament among a litter of puppies or kittens. From the moment we are born, the die is cast. Everything from eye colour, hair, height, weight, and intelligence to emotional makeup. Our genes also largely predetermine how we perceive and respond to the world around us. With the rise in DNA websites and people taking advantage of the knowledge they bring, we've learned how our genes dictate how we react to our environment. Ask any parent about their young, and they'll tell you each child she bears arrives with a unique disposition. They can be calm, agitated, cranky, or easy-going. Some sleep for hours on end, while others are challenging to settle.

This is not new information. The question of nature vs. nurture was debated over two thousand years ago, in Plato's and Aristotle's time. Plato favoured nature; Aristotle embraced nurture. Though

Aristotle once wrote, "In all things of nature, there is something of the marvellous."

In his 1874 book *English Men of Science: Their Nature and Nurture*, Francis Galton, a relative of Charles Darwin, notably wrote: "Nature and nurture is a convenient jingle of words, for it separates under two distinct heads the innumerable elements of which personality is composed. Nature is all that a man brings with himself into the world; nurture is every influence without that affects him after his birth."

Psychiatrists Alexander Thomas and Stella Chess noted the blame placed on mothers for child outcomes. In response, they launched the New York Longitudinal Study in 1956 to investigate infants' innate dispositions and their effect on long-term development, including personality, academic achievement, peer relationships, parent-child interactions, and mental health. They studied 138 middle-class white children and ninety-five lower-class Puerto Rican children from infancy to thirty-two years of age. They collected data on these individuals in childhood, adolescence, and young adulthood. It was an effort to determine how children contributed to their own development and identify whether and how child temperament interacts with the environment to produce specific outcomes.

They examined nine different personality traits: activity (the child's energy level); regularity (predictable or varied patterns for eating, sleeping, and going to the bathroom); initial reaction (open or hesitant in response to a new experience); adaptability (adaptable or resistant to change in their environment); intensity (exuberant

or lethargic); mood (naturally upbeat or downbeat); distractibili-
ty (attentive or sidetracked); persistence/attention span (immersed
or disinterested); sensory threshold (unaffected or irritated); and a
child's reaction to sensory stimuli (light, touch, smell, taste, heat,
cold, and pain).

They concluded that we don't come into the world with a blank
slate. We reveal our personalities right from the start.

This groundbreaking research project was discussed in *The
American Journal of Psychiatry*. The article begins with this sentence: "It is an unfortunate reality that life's unfairness starts at the
beginning of life." A powerful statement! It's clear that not everything is equal when we examine the traits a child is born with.

We come into this world with roots containing a hodgepodge of
genes—some stretching back many generations—that will influence
the path we take. Since we accept that eye and hair colour, musical
talent, mathematical ability, athletic prowess, and specific physical
health problems can be inherited, then why not come to terms with
the fact that other traits and vulnerabilities can also be passed down?

How often do we hear comments like: 'He's so much like his
mother,' 'She's just like her Aunt Lydia,' 'He's a chip off the old
block,' 'He's an optimist by nature,' and 'The apple doesn't fall far
from the tree.' There's obviously something about an individual's
behaviour that suggests some inherited quality.

More and more mental health professionals accept that genetics plays a major role in human and animal behaviour. One quick
Google search describes the possibilities for different breeds of pets,
from the shy, quiet, rambunctious, or inquisitive type to the one

clinging to their mother. Animal enthusiasts know there is a range of personalities in all litters. Yet, some in mental health keep arguing that the environment is the primary determinant of human behaviour.

If you come into the world with a few challenging personality traits and add to that unhealthy family dynamics, you have a heap of trouble to work through. It's the luck of the draw, whether your environment provides you with the love and nurture you need to make the best of the hand you've been given.

The Impact of Past Generations

Considerable research has been done to examine how a person's trauma affects their children and grandchildren. Through various studies, we know that specific life experiences will affect future descendants. Life-threatening events impact generations to come.

In the 1990s, I became aware of intergenerational trauma when I learned that one of my friends was a member of a support group for children of Holocaust survivors. Those whose parents and grandparents survived the Holocaust or any other genocide have different stress hormone profiles, perhaps predisposing them to anxiety disorders.

When I reflect on my childhood, I recall crying easily and often. And yet, my mother and grandmother, who lived with us, didn't shed tears. Though my mother didn't cry, she often talked about the hardship she and her family had endured as a Ukrainian living in Russia and Canada. When they immigrated here in 1929, they arrived in Manitoba just before the Great Depression began. As strangers in a hostile land, they weathered droughts, locusts, and prejudice for the next ten years. My father's eyes would glisten with tears when he heard those stories. I don't recall crying then, but the fact I cried easily and frequently led me to believe later in life that perhaps I did so because my mother and grandmother couldn't trust themselves to let a tear fall. I suspect they held back their emotions for fear they wouldn't be able to stop sobbing. So, I cried for them.

But maybe it wasn't fear of sinking into a depression that kept them from crying. Maybe they viewed crying as a sign of weakness. They worked long days and needed their strength to survive.

Either way, we know trauma affects our emotions. The shock of what we go through can shut us down. As is often the case with returning soldiers, they don't talk about what they've experienced on the battlefield. Like my mother and grandmother, they hold back. They don't want to break the dam they've erected. We say they are suffering from post-traumatic stress disorder. PTSD affects many who've experienced a life-threatening event.

Mark Wolynn, director of the Family Constellation Institute in San Francisco and a world leader in inherited family trauma, touches on this in his book *It Didn't Start with You: How Inherited Family Trauma Shapes Who We Are and How to End the Cycle.* He gives multiple examples of how a relative's trauma affects a family member's life a generation or two later.

The Missing Instruction Book

I recall becoming a young mother at only twenty when our first-born—a beautiful little girl—came along. I am an only child and had never babysat, so I had no experience with little ones. Though my husband had siblings and helped with the care of a much younger brother, he was an obedient and quiet child like me. I relied on the book *Dr. Spock's Baby and Child Care* and childhood memories to guide me. There wasn't today's flood of childcare books and resources back then. Our daughter was a spirited baby, and we learned much from her adventurous nature. She asserted herself from the beginning and made her voice known in no uncertain terms. We could've benefited from some outside guidance. Unfortunately, it was the sixties, and we knew no one who received help with raising their children. We were not great with discipline. We did our best and showered our daughter with love.

Wouldn't it be wonderful if parents got an instruction manual accompanying each childbirth? We get manuals for our household appliances and cars. And yet, we get nothing for the most important job of all—raising children. The manual for my Toyota Prius is immense. It's a car, not a human being, which is considerably more complex. Every owner—and there were 236,000 in Toyota Prius's best year—received the same manual. So, in all fairness, one manual meeting the needs of all humans would be a tall order because each human being is unique. We are still discovering how the brain works. Still, it would be helpful to at least get a printout for our babies based on their genetic makeup—like what we get on seed packets—so we are well-informed regarding what our child has in their DNA and what they will need to grow to their full potential. But since there is no manual, most of us rely on what we learned from our parents. We either repeat those lessons, wittingly or unwittingly, or go in another direction, all the while hoping to do what's best for our children.

In her inspiring book, *Braiding Sweetgrass: Indigenous Wisdom, Scientific Knowledge, and the Teachings of Plants,* botanist and author Robin Wall Kimmerer explores the relationship between humans and nature. Kimmerer encourages us to connect with nature and learn the lessons there. She writes, "There's a perfect little baby in every seed, blanketed in food, and protected in the seed coat." She goes further to celebrate the story held in every seed, which has everything it needs to begin life and go through cycles again. It even contains a memory of what the seed needs to start all over. But unlike the information we get from seed packets, we are not privy to what our babies carry into our world. Though we have an incomplete picture of them, we know they need love, understanding, and diligent care.

Our Nature

Our youngest daughter is a Waldorf teacher. Rudolf Steiner, a German educator, founded the Waldorf education model—a school of learning that recognizes four main temperaments, each responding to the environment in their own way.

Of course, there are variations to each temperament. Still, Steiner believed a teacher could use the four main types: melancholic (earth), phlegmatic (water), sanguine (air), and choleric (fire) as guidelines. These temperaments give Waldorf teachers a starting point—an idea of what each child might need to grow and develop. They are fluid and subject to change. What's important to understand is that each child comes into the world with predetermined characteristics—a fact that can't be overemphasized.

I recall our granddaughter jumping at the sound of a toilet flushing, a vacuum roaring, and fireworks exploding. Another grandchild—present at the same fireworks display—slept through the loudest bangs in the sky and easily dealt with other loud noises. Different children, different reactions.

Therapeutic circles have long overlooked how nature influences our behaviour. Back in the 1970s, I worked with a psychologist who had two autistic children. Therapists, who they sought for help, blamed him and his wife—a social worker—for their children's remote behaviour. As if they'd somehow caused autism. I saw nothing in their emotional makeup that suggested they would be less than loving parents. At a loss how to care for their children, they were encouraged to send them to a home for autistic kids in the United States. As devoted parents, they did what the therapists advised. How it must have broken their hearts to be blamed for their children's autism and then to be told they had to send them to a treatment home hundreds of miles away for their own good. It's not surprising then that they both suffered from depression after their children were taken from them. We've since learned that autism is not the cause of remote or cold parenting. Nature had played a leading role in their children's lives, leaving them helpless and downhearted.

New findings about the origins of autism came too late for the psychologist and his social worker wife. Autism is now recognized as a neurodevelopmental disorder and a developmental disability brought on by both environmental and biological factors. Because of genetics, the most nurturing parents can still have an autistic child.

To sum up, nature is what we come into the world with. We emerge from our mother's womb, not only with our physical and intellectual makeup but also with our temperament. How we emotionally respond to the world is part of our character. Some of our behaviour is within our control, but other traits cannot be curbed as easily.

As with the nature of a seed, it's impossible to change the nature of a human being. However, with nurture, we can modify the temperament we were born with. Someone who struggles with shyness can learn to overcome their timidity. It's not easy, but we can make great strides to overcome a predisposition to behave a certain way. Similarly, through nurture, rough edges can be softened. Just as the brain can build new pathways after trauma through physical exercise and nutrition, we can learn and adapt in an environment that provides love and care.

Nurture, Enhancing Nature

All living things need attention. Gardeners know seedlings need nurturing to get started. Mature plants need to be tended to as well. Our plants demand that we care for them—or they wilt and die. Same with humans.

Sir John Bowlby—a British psychoanalyst known for his pioneering work in attachment theory—wrote about the effects of maternal deprivation on child development. If the mother was unavailable to show any love and care in the first two years of a child's life, that infant would grow up insecure and have other emotional problems. There was even evidence that some babies died because they hadn't felt the human touch; they were not hugged or held.

Take two potted plants of the same type and place them side by side on the same windowsill. Give one nutrients and water, but ignore the other. Which one will thrive, and which one will perish? It can be as simple as that.

The human condition requires nurturing. Without it, we feel alone and unloved, regardless of age.

During the COVID pandemic, millions of elderly died. Because of the lockdown of long-term care facilities and hospital wards, they weren't allowed any visitors, even close family. I can't help but think that the lack of physical touch from loved ones hastened many of their deaths.

Love, acceptance, and understanding are critical to our well-being. When it's missing, we suffer. We can all think of someone in our lives, whether close or distant, who lost someone they loved because of a conflict or misunderstanding. It can be devastating. People fall into a depression they can't climb out of. Psychiatric wards are full of people who feel they have no one to turn to. Suicide and homicide are high among men whose relationships with their partners and family have been permanently severed. Among the homeless are many who've succumbed to drug addiction as a way of coping with their losses.

We show love to our plants by watering, feeding, and protecting them from wind and cold weather. We plant them in the shade or sun, depending on what they need to thrive. And we don't overcrowd them; we give them space to breathe and grow naturally.

We need to do the same with people. We need to pay attention and show our love. The Golden Rule, common to many faiths, "Love your neighbour as yourself," is worth heeding. This extends to family members, spouses, and lovers. If we ignore our family and friends, the potential for mutually beneficial relationships can evaporate as quickly as a puddle in the hot sun.

And most importantly, we need to love ourselves. It's difficult to love others when we don't nurture our own being. But depending on our uniqueness, beginnings, and road to adulthood, some of us are better prepared than others. When I think of those on the streets, I wonder how much of their plight stems from a lack of self-value?

If you grow up without love, your self-esteem naturally suffers. If you're told often enough that you're stupid, selfish, mean, or 'a piece of shit,' you can imagine the damage.

Demeaning language cuts us deeply. It takes a lot to recover from verbal and emotional abuse. If someone you love stiffens at your touch every time you hug them, what does that convey? Does it tell you that you count in their eyes? There are many ways we can hurt others close to us. We can reject them with a single look, gesture, or word.

It makes me think of a middle-aged woman who had been admitted for depression to the psychiatric ward at the Winnipeg General Hospital. She had stopped eating and going to work. When she refused to get out of bed, her husband and two young children had to fend for themselves. The psychiatric team learned she had received a letter from her father, who lived in Greece, accusing her of being a neglectful daughter, the uncaring one in the family, the selfish one. Berated since she was young, she felt the sting of her father's letter. It took little to open old wounds. Though the letter had the power to hurt her deeply, she needed to learn how to nurture herself even when she was being attacked. She needed help to deal with the hurt she had bottled up, the hurt that was weighing her down.

Finding Nurture in Your Community

How much nurture we get from our community became apparent during the COVID pandemic. Many who went through the crisis found it tough to be suddenly cut off from their school, work, community, and social network. And yet, there was solace for many when they found themselves stuck indoors with their families. Parents found that the extra time at home with their offspring had both benefits and challenges. Some families grew closer together, but others suffered because of the increased opportunities for conflict. There was no escape. If their own kin were unavailable or lacking in support, they missed those they had embraced outside of it—their adopted families.

During the pandemic, we were somewhat saved because of the power of the internet. It allowed us to connect with others via Zoom, Google Meet, Skype, WhatsApp, and other online services which allowed us to see their faces and hear their voices. The smiles we saw online helped to ease the pain of isolation.

The loss of meaningful connection during this period reminded us of the role it plays in maintaining our psychological and spiritual well-being. For those suffering from loneliness, depression, and anxiety, therapists often recommend getting involved with others through community centres, faith groups, and volunteer work. Though we may be introverted by nature, it doesn't mean it's what we want or need. A smile from someone, even a stranger, goes a long way, as do simple exchanges (like 'Good Day,' 'How are you?' and 'Thank you'). Even a comment on the weather helps. Before long, a conversation may flow, providing the human connection most need.

Recently, I went for a walk on a fishing pier close to home, where I had a lovely encounter with a young boy who was about twelve years old. He was holding a fishing rod and bending his head over the rail. I asked him if he could see any fish. He said, "Sometimes."

I asked him what he was catching. "Green fingerlings, but I throw them back in. I don't keep them. They have feelings."

His response surprised me. Fingerlings are baby fish, but he was already aware of the sensitivity of all creatures, even the tiny ones.

He added, "The fishermen I talk to don't think the fish they catch have any brains. But they do."

"You wouldn't keep any fish?" I asked.

Looking over at me, he said, "Well, if it's a salmon or cod, I might eat it."

I asked him where he learned all this. He shrugged, then said, "Nature is mental health."

Wow, I thought. *A wise young person.* I appreciated that he was engaging with Nature in such a sensitive way. I said, "It was nice talking to you." He smiled and said the same. A simple hello led to a pleasing conversation for the both of us. My small exchange with the young lad a few blocks from home made my day. There are so many opportunities to connect, if only we take the time to seek them.

Granted, there are many who prefer their own company, a quiet time away from the chaos of their lives. That can be an invaluable opportunity to reflect on their choices, plan their projects, consider their next steps. I also enjoy the tranquil times when I walk alone in the forest or along the seawall not far from our home. Any break from routine can revitalize our being. But if we avoid social interactions of any kind and our only company is our thoughts, they can lead us to dark or boring places. It's much like living in a house with all the windows shut. There's no avenue for fresh air to get in.

It is rare to see a plant growing far from others. Before long, the wind or a bird will drop another seed near it, and soon, the soil is covered in green growth. Nature is full of examples of various plants living in harmony. They have a community they can depend on for company.

In the last decade, we've seen many books showing us how trees, fungi, and other vegetation help one another thrive, even when they're under attack by insects or drought. They issue warnings and spread them through the forest. These are notable example of how species in nature rely on one another to survive and thrive.

Finding Nurture in Nature

In the 1980s, the Japanese government instituted the practice of *forest bathing*. It recognized that workers in society with their strong work ethic were experiencing burnout. The stress in their daily lives had taken its toll; too many were suffering. To deal with their high work demands, the Japanese government encouraged citizens to soothe themselves and replenish their spirits by taking walks in the forest.

Other urban cultures have also embraced a form of forest therapy, such as self-guided nature trails with markers instructing participants to take a deep breath, close their eyes, and listen to the forest sounds. They are also encouraged to stop and smell the vegetation surrounding them.

Researchers have studied the physiological benefits of ecotherapy—activities done in Nature to soothe our spirits and quieten our restless minds. Studies show that time spent in natural surroundings calms the mind; it makes people less anxious, less stressed, and less irritable. There are even courses people can take to get a certificate as a Forest Therapy Guide—a growing occupation.

There is something about a walk in the forest that soothes my senses. My mind is constantly whirling with what I've written and what I want to write, as well as regular family business—both joys and worries. However, in the forest's air, my mind tunes into bird-song and the sun's glory on the leaves of trees. A visit to Nature allows me to replenish my spirit and press pause on my concerns.

The quote: "Study Nature, love Nature, stay close to Nature. It will never fail you," is commonly attributed to Frank Lloyd Wright, the groundbreaking architect who designed buildings with the natural environment in mind. Anyone viewing his work can see the role Nature played in his creativity.

In the Netflix documentary *Live to 100, Secrets of the Blue Zones*, Nature also plays a leading role. Blue Zones are places in the world known for their low rates of chronic disease and high life expectancy. If you want to live to be one hundred and beyond, gardening helps as a hobby. The nonagenarians (people in their nineties) and centenarians (those one hundred and older) in the Blue Zones of Sardinia, Italy, and Okinawa, Japan, spend part of their day gardening. Caring for the plants gives them fresh air, physical exercise in the form of natural movement, time to escape their troubling thoughts and reduce stress, and vegetables for plant-based diets. They live in a community that fosters this activity, which promotes their mental health.

You don't have to live in a Blue Zone to include the beneficial practice of gardening in your daily life. If you live in a condo with a balcony, you can grow vegetables and plants in pots. And for those who don't have outdoor space, even one plant to care for can do wonders for shut-ins. When you can't get to Nature, you can bring it indoors. Taking care of a plant and watching it grow can be very rewarding. It can give purpose to those who live alone and have few social contacts.

Plants and trees rely on one another for help during a drought or an infestation. Similarly, we need to rely on those we care about and those who care about us. And yet, with our busy lives, we sometimes neglect to nurture our relationships. We need to take time to nurture them and ourselves. Connecting with those we love is one way of doing that. Gardening is another.

The Garden Plan

LIFE'S A GARDEN

We begin planning what we want from life long before we can be on our own. We think about careers, marriage, and family when we are young. We play with dolls, trucks, and blocks, imagining ourselves in various roles through play.

All our decisions are filtered through family expectations and our own dreams. What do I want to be when I grow up? Will I attend university or college? Where will I live? Do I want to get married? Who will I marry? Do I want to have children? The questions are the same with every generation. There are so many choices, so many decisions.

When we plan a flower or a vegetable garden, we control where a seed or a plant will be planted. We can take soil bereft of nutrients and add what is needed. Or we can dig it all out and start afresh. Either way, we're making a change for the better. We've recognized that what we have isn't working, and we've embarked on improving our garden.

When I look to my garden for inspiration, I see shallow flower beds and a lot of sandy soil. Because I'm not a fussy gardener, the plants that go into my garden must be hardy. I don't run out and pull the first weed that raises its unwelcome head. Because I'm a writer preoccupied with words, I fuss just enough with my garden to make it pleasing to the eye. It blooms almost year-round and attracts birds, bees, and butterflies. Forests surround the small city I live in, so it's not unusual to have deer visit and rest for a while, then stand to nibble on our viburnum hedge. I welcome them but keep a mindful eye. I don't want them to eat all the leaves. A little of their pruning during a surprise visit is fine.

When planning your life's garden, it helps to look at what you have to work with, much like assessing what's needed for a pleasing landscape. Knowing your own nature, you could ask yourself: What life do I envision for myself? What are my priorities? What do I need to plant in my life to give me joy and comfort?

It helps to start with your basic needs.

Maslow's Hierarchy of Needs

No matter what kind of family we come from, we are all united in our basic needs.

In 1943, American psychologist Abraham Maslow developed a theory of human motivation, which is still used today. Maslow's Hierarchy of Needs (1943) is often depicted as a pyramid.

At a minimum, we need food, water, shelter, warmth, sex, sleep, and clean air. Next, we need to feel safe. That means protection from the elements, comfort in knowing there is law and order in our lives, and stability in our environment.

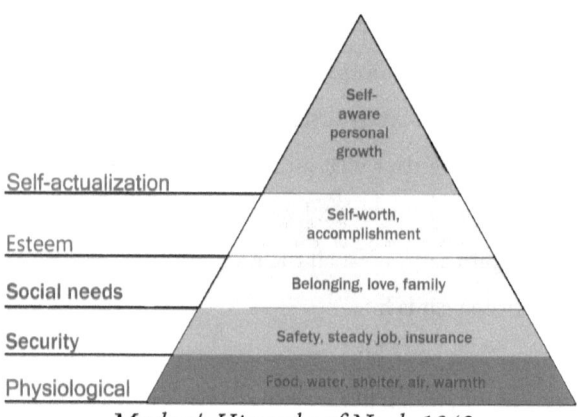

Maslow's Hierarchy of Needs 1943

Once those basic needs are met, many will be content. But invariably, other concerns may crop up. When we begin our life's journey, we don't know what we will do well, so we experiment. Just as we change plants and their location to please our eye and palate when growing our garden, we assess and review what works for us in life.

We're also creatures who need a sense of belonging, which comes from our human connections: our families, colleagues, and friends. Love and attachment come from belonging, connecting with others, and being intimate with a caring partner. Is this something you're nurturing? Are you putting in the time to stay in touch? How much connection do you need?

But having that emotional security isn't enough. We also need to feel as though we are the masters of our own fate. We need independence and a sense of accomplishment. We crave to master a craft and gain prestige or high social status. We study, take courses, or complete other training. Or we learn a trade. For those who aren't tired after a day's work, there are multiple avenues for developing a new skill: joining a choir, taking a painting course, enrolling in a cooking class, signing up for a sport, and doing volunteer work.

In the 1970s, Maslow added a few more needs. He believed we also have cognitive needs; we need to know and understand. We want predictability and meaning in our lives. We are all curious creatures at heart, some more so than others. For example, pursuing and appreciating beauty, balance, and form can lead to personal self-fulfilment. We can also satisfy this cognitive need by studying, travelling, and reading.

Maslow's additions were a response to societal changes. As mentioned earlier, the seventies were called the 'Me Decade.' The general population began to reflect on who they were, what they wanted out of life, how they could actualize their goals, and improve themselves. Having gone through the Great Depression, the older folks couldn't understand why young people spent so much time contemplating their lives. They'd been too busy working around the clock to consider how life could be different for them.

But with shorter workdays and weeks, there was now time to examine oneself. Popular self-help books became the rage. Some standouts: *Looking Out for #1* by Robert Ringer, *Pulling Your Own Strings* by Dr. Wayne W. Dyer, *How to Be Your Own Best Friend* by Mildred Newman et al., *Passages: Predictable Crises of Adult Life* by Gail Sheehy, *What Colour Is Your Parachute* by Richard Nelson Bolles, and *The Road Less Traveled* by M. Scott Peck. The titles speak for themselves.

When There's A Crisis

For many, time for introspection only comes when there's a crisis. It's obvious that something needs to be done when our lives are in upheaval and we don't know which way to turn. Adversity challenges us in every way—emotionally, psychologically, and physically. We can be pulled into the abyss of 'woe is me.' And certainly, some life events are not easily overcome. They require time to process. Though it can be a challenging time, it can also be an opportunity for change. The Chinese symbols for crisis translate to danger and a change point. The news is full of stories about people who've had near-death experiences that affected them so deeply they changed the way they approached their daily lives. Their crisis was a wake-up call. It caused them to take the time to re-evaluate the choices they had made. They accepted their vulnerability; they took note of the fragility of life.

The COVID pandemic, which lasted several years, had a similar effect on many. Some people started a new business or changed their jobs. Others made a big move from the city, where the cost of living is high, to towns in other provinces or states, where they felt less pressured financially. Where there's a will, there's a way.

And then there were those who appreciated the slower pace. They didn't have to rush into the office and deal with traffic jams. They appreciated the stillness of the forests where they could hear the birds sing for the first time. The pandemic gave them the opportunity to reflect on their values, what they wanted out of life.

When in crisis, we become immobilized or mobilized to do something different. If we take the time to reflect on what's happening, we can examine what's working and what's not more critically. If we cannot do so because we are too distraught, a therapist may be of help.

What Roots Tell Us

Roots travel deep to gather the water and nutrients plants need to thrive. They keep a plant in place, protecting it from strong winds and soil erosion. When roots can spread and grow without constraint, the plant flourishes. Similarly, when we can grow without restraint and actualize our potential, we also flourish.

Like planning a garden, we need to assess what we have to work with. There's no one right place to start, but a good one is your family tree. What's in your seed? How strong are your roots? How strong are your branches? With the rise of interest in genealogy, people worldwide have been exploring their roots—their parents' origins and those who came before them.

Our Family of Origin

Exploring your family of origin is instructive. It could be a traditional one with a mother, a father, and children. Or one headed by a single parent. Maybe there were extended family members living with you. If your family home was a multi-generational one, how did that affect your status? Were you the oldest, the youngest, or the middle child? Or an only child? Were you a surprise or illegitimate?

Did your parents have to get married because of an unplanned pregnancy? If they did, how did you find out? Did they expect a girl or a boy? If you were adopted, what do you know about that story? In many families, there are often stories that still reverberate decades later.

It's the luck of the draw, whether we are born into a wealthy family or one that's barely making ends meet. We might be the only child to a woman whose partner is long gone, a child adopted at birth, or the last of four children. We have no control over our race, sexuality, or religion. Of course, we can change the latter if we choose to do so when we're older, but in the early years, we are influenced by what our parents believe and what we are exposed to. No matter where we live, we grow up using the script our family unconsciously wrote. That script includes manners, expectations, values, and how we are supposed to relate to people within and outside our family.

Family stories unearth more than birth and death dates, the names of couples, the number of children, and so on. Examining one's family tree may expose the strengths and the vulnerabilities within it. They uncover illnesses and causes of death. One family might have a history of mental illness, another of alcoholism, a third of heart problems and high blood pressure, a fourth of cancer or diabetes, and so on. These are the big health issues, but there are others worth noting, especially if there's a pattern repeated by other family members. A susceptibility to physical ailments can be passed on, which is why doctors often ask questions about the health of other family members.

In discussing the family tree, some therapists also pay attention to family cut-offs. They explore why one family member is no longer talking to another and how this affects family dynamics and the person seeking help. Therapists consider if there were any attempts to repair the relationship and the results of those efforts.

Our Genetic Blueprint

We can now access more health information through our DNA—the genetic blueprint, which dictates more than we think, such as information about possible hereditary conditions that hadn't been revealed in family stories. Those digging into their ancestral roots through online services like Ancestry.com learn about any health risks and vulnerabilities they might have.

If any of your ancestors struggled with addiction, drugs, or alcohol, it's worth considering, as there are some schools of thought that view addiction as hereditary. If you or someone close to you develops a habit of consuming several drinks daily or shows a high tolerance for alcohol, it would be wise to explore whether they have a genetic predisposition to becoming addicted.

It bears underlining that just because you discover serious illness or other susceptibilities in your family tree, it doesn't mean you'll succumb to any of it yourself. With a good diet, exercise, and other positive lifestyle choices, there's a lot you can do to stay mentally and physically healthy. Though you can't always prevent illness, knowing more about your family tree can help you identify what you need to do to raise the odds in your favour. Fortunately, we now live in a time when new treatments tackle the scariest diagnoses and extend life way beyond what was possible a generation or two ago. Still, no one wants to gamble with their health. As they say, being forewarned is being forearmed.

Inherited Family Trauma

As mentioned earlier, parents, grandparents, and other ancestors can pass down their emotional pain through family anecdotes and other behaviour. Many children of Holocaust survivors absorb their family's traumatic past and thus sign up to be in support groups to talk about what they know and how that genocide affected them. As well, we've become aware of Indigenous communities labouring through the burden of what their elders have gone through as children in residential schools and other effects of colonization. The trauma shows up in the high suicide rate among the young and the high incidence of drug and alcohol addiction.

Exploring our family tree helps us examine the past, as it often explains why we do what we do, think what we think, and feel what we feel. Knowing that family trauma can be passed on, it's not surprising then that many get triggered by news, life events, or conversations that bring up the pain of the past.

An example of family pain passed on through generations happened when Russia invaded Ukraine in 2022. Like many in the Ukrainian diaspora, I went into shock when I heard the news. I sobbed uncontrollably. Though I was born to Ukrainian immigrants in Winnipeg, Manitoba, over a half-century earlier, I was surprised by my reaction and wondered why I had reacted so strongly. Ukraine wasn't my birthplace, and yet Russia's invasion had wounded me. Our family has some second and third cousins in Ukraine, but we had lost touch with them decades earlier. There was no one I could call and yet I felt as if my immediate family was under attack. After some introspection, I realized there were good reasons why the invasion had torn me apart emotionally. One, I was still writing my Ukrainian grandmother's family saga set in Canada, Poland, Ukraine, and Russia. I was on book three of the trilogy when the war began. All these family tales—the voices of my mother and grandmother in my head—contributed to my depression. I knew what hardships my baba and her children had endured in the old country and how they had been treated by the Russians in authority. And two, Ukraine is in my blood; the country's history is in my DNA. My depression was short-lived, but my grief was undeniable.

As of this writing, Ukraine continues to fight Russia for its sovereignty and independence; it fears being swept under its neighbour's mighty thumb. Its tormented history under Russia's rule goes back centuries. The harshest time was during the *Holodomor,* Stalin's government-sponsored famine of 1932-33, which killed millions. The horror of that genocide still weighs heavily on the minds of Ukrainians, especially those with ancestors who had experienced loss and deprivation during that devastating period of Russia's history.

We are the offspring of our fathers and mothers who inherited trauma from their parents and passed it down the line. Just because we don't know their specific traumas doesn't mean it hasn't infiltrated our being, colouring who we are.

The Strength of Your Roots

Though you can do little about the past, you can do something about your future by examining your current situation and the direction you've taken in life. How strong are the roots you've put down? How strongly do you feel about what's happened to you in the past? Does criticism from family, friends, teachers, and others still haunt you and affect how you handle other slights? Do harsh words from ex-partners make you wary of forming other loving relationships? How much do you trust in your environment? What do you need to put in place to thrive and feel secure?

Patterns and Habits

F amily patterns are often repeated from one generation to the next. We come into the world helpless and rely on the family who raises us. We follow their example as if by osmosis.

We can find obvious examples of this in the animal kingdom. As with ducks and geese, a newborn calf follows their mother's lead, which is called imprinting. Naturally, the young are susceptible to copying the behaviour of those who care for them. Their parents are often the first beings they see when they open their eyes.

Whether we realize it or not, we adopt healthy and unhealthy patterns from those closest to us.

I recall one couple who came to see me for marital therapy. Concerned about their six-year-old son, the wife had coaxed her husband to come, even though he had already decided to leave their marriage. He'd found another relationship, which he believed would answer his needs. Though he was initially reluctant to fully participate in the counselling session, I carried on as if he was committed to healing the rift with his wife. I drew a genogram giving a snapshot of his family tree and another of hers. A genogram is a visual diagram showing a limited family tree—the nuclear family, siblings, parents, and grandparents with their medical history and other concerning behaviours.

In the husband's genogram, I discovered a family pattern he was thinking of repeating. His father had left his mother when he was six. It had traumatized him, but it was a trauma he had buried. He had never connected his wish to leave his marriage—when his own son was six—with his unresolved grief over his father deserting the family. He had never talked with his wife or anyone else about the range of emotions he had gone through at the time—abandonment, anger, frustration, helplessness, and sorrow. Once he saw the connection, he could talk openly about his pain and begin to heal with his wife's help. In the end, he stayed in his marriage and broke the unhealthy pattern of running away when he felt he was losing control.

Another example comes to mind. I had a client who was so sensitive he erupted in anger at his wife whenever he thought she was mocking him, like when they played tennis. Jan was an excellent player, and their matches were usually evenly matched. Grant would win one game, she'd crush another. But almost every time she was on a winning streak, he became frustrated and reacted by swearing or hitting the ball hard toward her. Surprised by his behaviour, she laughed out of stress. Winning seemed so important to him. She considered not bothering to try so hard and letting him win. But having grown up with the notion of equality of the sexes, she didn't want to do that. She also thought that could be insulting to him. Winning because your opponent isn't trying hard would not be satisfying in the end. She also knew that despite his obvious frustration, Grant also believed in the equality of the sexes.

With help from a marital therapist, they learned that Jan was unknowingly triggering memories of the times Grant's brother had mocked him when they were teens competing in various sports. He could never beat his brother. He wouldn't have minded losing, except his brother taunted him, and his parents praised his brother's skills. As a result, Grant grew up feeling inadequate. He kept trying to prove to himself he was good enough.

In Grant's case, both he and his wife had habits to break while playing tennis together. Awareness helped change Jan's reaction. When Grant reacted badly to a missed shot, she no longer viewed it as funny. She also talked to him about wanting to play her best and discussed whether he really wanted her to let him win if she could honestly beat him. This helped Grant realize it was just a game, not a judgment on his adequacy as a man.

Becoming Mindful of Unhealthy Patterns

We are all creatures of habit. It helps to have a healthy routine. But sometimes, the patterns we adopt become unhealthy and hard to break.

Many of us note the bad ones on New Year's Eve. We make resolutions: We'll stop biting our fingernails, we'll stop smoking, we'll reach out to the friends we've neglected, we'll call Mom more often, we'll try not to react and be so sensitive, we'll start exercising, we'll eat less, we'll give up candy, alcohol, or drugs. The list is endless.

Our addiction to social media is an unhealthy habit making the news, even inciting our politicians to make bold statements. It's an epidemic unfolding around the globe. Glued to their devices, young children have been affected socially, emotionally, and physically. In generations past, they would be too busy running and playing outdoors with their friends 'till the streetlights came on. Instead of active play in their community, kids these days are consumed with video games, social media, and messaging. They sit, stand, lie down, and even sleep with their devices. Social media—like TikTok and Instagram—is seductive and addictive. We've seen countless photos and videos of young people standing beside each other in theatre line-ups or outside their schools with their eyes glued to their screens. Even on family road trips, parents will find the young staring at their cellphones or tablets instead of taking in the scenery outside their car windows.

The people who run the apps know precisely how to seduce us because they analyze our viewing habits. That data helps them respond with images and reels they know we'll like. They want us to remain transfixed by our screens so they can insert ads and capitalize on their investment. It's easy to become so absorbed that we overlook the need to exercise, get a good night's sleep, or make a nourishing meal.

Technology was supposed to be a time saver, but it's become anything but. It gobbles up our time, robbing us of face-to-face dates with friends and family, substituting pictures and videos for real-time phone calls. It keeps us indoors, slumped on our bed or living room couch.

Then, there are habits that go too far. In the film *As Good as It Gets,* actor Jack Nicholson portrays a man stuck in his habits and struggling with an obsessive-compulsive disorder. It paralyzes him and keeps him from having a normal social life. We laugh at his predicament and obnoxious behaviour, but also empathize with those he hurts. We understand his compulsion, but it's hard to accept. There is pain not only for the ones who suffer from compulsive habits but also for those who have to deal with them.

Some of us may have a psychological disorder without realizing it. We all adopt patterns, from our sleep habits to our diet to our temperament in daily life. Some are healthy, others are not. Everyone has debris in their life, stuff from the past—an unhappy childhood, a broken marriage, a friendship gone sour—that they've carried into the present. There is no life without trials and tribulations. Couple that with our inherited vulnerabilities, and it's no wonder many struggle to find happiness and love.

There are some things we can change and some we cannot. We are greater than the sum of our parts, including memories of the past and buried feelings. But no matter the journey, there is a way forward. There is hope to improve the hand we've been dealt. We can develop better habits. Awareness is the first step in changing the behaviours that no longer serve us.

Weeding

THE MANY FACES OF DEPRESSION

A t some point in our lives, we all suffer from a form of depression. It's unavoidable. It's part of life's ups and downs. It can go as quickly as it comes, but there are times when it can stay so long it affects not only our daily functioning but also the well-being of those who care about us.

Therapists recognize many faces of depression. Depression can be triggered by the death of a loved one, job loss, divorce, heartbreak, betrayal, bullying, world events, or other adversity. Or it could be biological, caused by inherited traits, perhaps stemming from an imbalance of neurotransmitters, chronic stress, or childhood trauma. Perhaps the depression is more psychological and brought on by feelings of failure, unrealistic expectations, or negative self-talk, while others become disillusioned when they realize that achieving goals they've been chasing their whole life won't bring them happiness. Doctors today also recognize that some women get depressed the week before their menstrual cycle begins. Though it may not last long each month, it can debilitate, especially when it consistently interferes with their mood.

Psychiatrists today have new names for the various types, but regardless of the category, depression can be simply viewed as a mood disorder that causes a lengthy period of sadness and loss of interest. The depressed can feel sad, empty or irritable and unable to function at work and at home. Most depressive disorders develop from a combination of biological, psychological, and environmental factors.

Adjustment Disorder with Depressed Mood

Adjustment Disorder with Depressed Mood is the new term for what was once termed as a situational depression. It's a depression that's common to many. It's natural to feel sad, especially after the death of a loved one, the loss of job, divorce, heartbreak, bullying, or other adversity. Fortunately, most recover with time. Often, recovery depends on the emotional support available from family, friends, and/or one's faith. The amount of time grieving also matters.

For example, Jewish people ease their suffering after the death of a loved one by performing the ritual of sitting shiva. For seven days, they sit at home and grieve. During this mourning process, family and friends bring food to comfort them; they talk and share stories of the deceased. This kind of acknowledgement and emotional support does much to ease a mourner's pain.

It takes time to heal. No matter what faith one carries, the support of others helps immeasurably. If someone becomes immobilized because of their grief, that's the time to seek professional help. If they're unmotivated, their physician might refer them to a psychiatrist who can prescribe anti-depressants to help kick start the treatment process. Then, with the guidance of a therapist, the depressed can work through the grief weighing them down. They can talk through their pain and release emotions, perhaps crying and sharing feelings of anger, sadness, or guilt.

According to Elisabeth Kubler-Ross—a Swiss-born American psychiatrist who studied the depression that people develop following the death of a loved one—there are five stages of grief: denial, anger, bargaining, depression, and acceptance. Not everyone goes through all five stages, and there are variations in each one.

Understandably, the first reaction seems to be denial when there is any kind of loss or impending loss. Why is this happening to me? It must be a mistake. If it's a medical issue, we think the doctors are wrong, and we'll wake up from this nightmare. Was something overlooked? Can we do anything differently to change our future?

Anger follows denial. We're frustrated. We naturally think life is unfair and look for someone to blame. We rail against the world or those close to us.

The third stage is bargaining. We pray and ask God for help. We promise to change, if only what's happening can be reversed.

And then, when nothing we do changes the loss we face, we slip into depression. We give up. All is lost. There's no way out of this grief.

The final stage is acceptance. This is when we begin to heal ourselves and work through the grief. We take responsibility for change.

It's challenging when a family member is depressed for long periods and shows an inability to let go of their pain. Sometimes guilt, anger, or hurt complicates that sadness. For example, when a child passes away, grieving parents may blame themselves for not recognizing their child's illness or state of mind sooner and not acting soon enough to prevent their death.

The story of a woman I'll call Marion has stayed with me all these years. She lost her son to drug addiction—or, more specifically, violence. Whoever he owed money to fatally stabbed him in a local park at night. Marion spent countless hours reviewing the steps she'd taken to help her son overcome his drug addiction and found her efforts lacking. She kept going over his childhood, trying to figure out where she went wrong. Or what she and his father could have done differently. She visited her son's grave daily, talking to him, trying to make peace, but also trying to show him—as if he was still alive—how much she cared. She would have endless one-sided conversations with her deceased son, explaining herself and apologizing for being so blind. Though she had a husband and two other children at home, her life was so wrapped up in guilt and sorrow she could not step outside herself to see how much her family needed her. When her husband tried to console her and suggested she had to move on, she turned on him, raging that he didn't care about the son who had died.

Marion's depression cast a shadow over the whole family. Everyone felt hurt. She held a lot of power in her family—which was difficult for other family members to shake. Blinded by her protracted grief, Marion could not see how her actions were affecting others. She was unknowingly keeping her family hostage and preventing them from moving forward. And since she was unwilling to go for help, the best they could do was get help themselves.

Within a family, the one garnering the most attention is usually forced to break the cycle of unhealthy behaviour when other members change their actions. Not everyone chooses a healthier path. If they're unable or unwilling to do so, at least others can find solace in one another and get on with their lives.

Major Depressive Disorder

A major depressive disorder (MDD) doesn't appear to have any external cause. Instead, it seems to be caused by biological or genetic factors. It is a severe melancholy.

A therapist looking at a patient's family tree may discover other members who've been diagnosed with depression in the past. For example, a dentist who came to see me expressed fears his depression was taking him down a dark road. When I drew his genogram, I found that several men in his family tree had committed suicide. My client had identified warning signs and wisely came in for help. Through my encouragement, he went to his family doctor, who then referred him to a psychiatrist for medication and hopefully, follow-up psychotherapy.

This type of depression is often treated with anti-depressants and, in some persistent cases, electroconvulsive therapy (ECT). Though some have heralded ECT as the treatment that works when all else fails, many claim it's stolen the lives they once had. Their memories have forever been affected. After undergoing ECT, the author Ernest Hemingway famously said, "What these shock treatments did was they made a mess of my memory... They gave me a very bad time and they're not done yet." He believed the shock treatments had tampered with both his ability to remember things and his creativity, making it challenging for him to write. Though cured of what ailed him before the treatment, he became depressed over what he had lost in the process. Not long after, he committed suicide.

In 1972, I was stunned to see ECT routinely prescribed for seriously depressed patients in the psychiatric ward where I worked. I was naïve at the time and believed that what patients needed was empathy from a therapist, time to tell their stories and release their pain, and support to find contentment in life again. For some, this approach may work, but for those who remain locked in their misery, medication with timely follow-up and psychotherapy is the answer. But even then, some psychiatrists will argue, patients need more than that and that is when shock therapy is prescribed.

As mentioned earlier, the psych ward, where I worked, was a short-stay hospital unit; there was pressure from the administration to find a treatment that worked quickly to free up hospital beds. And ECT did just that. It worked quickly, but it only gave temporary relief to those suffering. In almost every case, they had to return for more treatments when depression raised its ugly head again. And with each subsequent treatment, they sunk further into the shadows of their former selves. All too often, the patients sat in family meetings with heads bent and slumped shoulders, as if they were carrying a heavy load.

Emotionally affected by what I had witnessed, I wrote a screenplay about a psychiatric intern who's up against the system. When my agent couldn't find a producer willing to option my screenplay and make a movie, I rewrote it as a novel. Set in 1972, my book shows both sides of the argument—for and against ECT—in the conflict between supervising psychiatrist Dr. Myron Eisenstadt and his passionate intern Dr. Joanna Bereza. After reading my novel, a former psychiatric patient asked me to join a group of ECT survivors on Facebook, where countless members share their frustration and grief over having gone through such treatments. One woman who used to have a well-paying administrative job in business complained that she was now working in the stockroom of T.J. Maxx, and even those simple tasks were hard for her. Others in the Facebook group were suing their healthcare providers for damages.

However, there are also many stories about people who've been saved by shock treatment, which has improved markedly over the past few decades. Feeling suicidal, they had tried drugs and exercise, but when those measures failed to lift their dark clouds, they consented to ECT. Though their depression wasn't completely erased after a series of treatments, they no longer felt like killing themselves. They could now lead a more normal life. Electro-convulsive therapy is still considered a last resort, as it has to be administered with care to avoid any physical damage. As well, stigma from the past continues to haunt its application. And so, the debate continues over the efficacy of ECT treatment.

Anger Management

A nger is a complex emotion. When people are angry, they may not know what has upset them. Is it some hurt, disappointment, fear, humiliation, frustration, or unresolved grief? Anger often masks deeper and less comfortable feelings, such as sorrow and fear. Much conflict can be avoided if we take a deep breath and pause or walk away instead of responding in kind.

Most of us have been taught to use our words, not fists. But even so, words can cut like knives. When we're attacked (verbally or physically) or feel threatened, the natural physiological response is to fight back, flee, or freeze. Though this is a natural reaction, we need to take responsibility for what we say and do. Depending on our personality and how often we've felt slighted, we will act out or retreat or become immobilized in different ways.

Unresolved Trauma

Unresolved trauma can also trigger the fight, flight, or freeze reaction repeatedly. The person reacting may not remember the original traumatic event, but the body remembers and reacts accordingly to what it perceives as a threat. Psychiatrist, Dr. Bessel Van der Kolk writes about this in depth in his well-received book, *The Body Keeps the Score.*

We feel horrified when we read about people who've lost control of their anger. It's difficult for most of us to understand. But when we learn the history of the persons involved and the details of the conflict, we begin to understand how a disagreement may have snowballed.

To illustrate the extremes of anger in my anger management workshops, I would draw a long horizontal line with suicide written at one end, and homicide at the other. I did it not to scare anyone, but to show the range of that human emotion. The line represented anger on a continuum—from repressed anger (held) to expressed anger (pushed out). Most people manage to avoid these extremes. They find ways to express their feelings without hurting anyone; they avoid doing or saying anything that contributes to the problem. They stop before the conflict gets out of hand.

But this is not the case for those who go too far. We know that those who commit suicide have been sitting on a pile of hurts, often ones they haven't shared. They had kept their thoughts and emotions to themselves. They had stewed and stewed over life, but all inwardly. Some even leave an angry note behind. Even more concerning are those who commit homicide; their anger is a 3D, cinematic, over-the-top explosion of emotion. Like the ones who commit suicide, they had let their anger build. Blind with rage, they lost complete control and lashed out in violent ways. Tragically in these cases, their families are often blindsided, not knowing how to reach their troubled loved one and help them deal with their pain.

Anger management means managing the thorns that accumulate and pierce goodwill. It means sharing the pain and dealing with perceived slights. When an emotional wound is allowed to fester for a long time, there's a build-up of resentment, which comes with an unwillingness to consider the other side. All too often, both parties dig their heels in.

Stepping Back

It is wise to take time to cool off in any conflict. I realize this is difficult for many, especially when emotions are high. Communication of any kind is further complicated if either party is under the influence of drugs or alcohol. Heated words or actions can easily trigger the fight, flight, or freeze response. But stepping back allows our emotions to settle so we can see the situation clearly. We can't think straight when we're feeling emotionally upset.

If you are one who keeps your feelings to yourself because there's no one in your circle you can trust to understand, then see a counsellor. Going for therapy, even if it's brief, gives you an opportunity to get what's troubling you off your chest and mind. Unburdening yourself makes you feel less alone; it creats space in your thinking to come up with ways to deal with a difficult situation or relationship.

As a consultant in emotional and behavioural problems in the classroom, I often talked to teachers about the value of using a *time-out* with so-called troublemakers—those who create chaos and disrupt lessons because they hit a classmate, act disrespectfully, damage school property, or break stuff. In the early grades, teachers set aside a space for a disruptive child to calm down and consider what had led to the *timeout* and reflect on their behaviour.

Giving a *timeout* with gentle firmness, clarity, and understanding can be very effective. However, this needs to be done with sensitivity to all involved. Isolating a child can be seen as shaming and punitive by both the child and their classmates. The debate today is over those adults who use it as punishment, demeaning and humiliating the misbehaving child in the process.

Today, there are additional strategies, like restorative justice, to manage the situation. Instructors implementing restorative justice look at ways to help both the acting-out student and the injured party rebuild their relationship and cultivate a sense of community. Though taking a breather is still encouraged, the child may be asked to come into the group rather than sit outside of it. They are given the opportunity to repair the harm. The values of empathy, respect, and understanding for all are promoted by those in charge.

When emotions rule and anger escalates to violence, a teacher can't teach. All attention goes to the troublesome child. When educators do nothing and the disruptive child gains the upper hand, every student in the classroom suffers. It bears repeating—it isn't healthy for any child to have that kind of power. Children need boundaries, especially when they are so young. They feel protected and cared for when rules are clear and the consequences for breaking them are spelled out.

But if the child in question seriously harms another or damages school property or a classmate's belongings, then parents have to be involved. Together with the teacher, they can work on ways to help the rebellious child, which might entail individual or family therapy.

The Straw That Broke the Camel's Back

When it comes to unintended slights, how people respond depends on their sensitivity. Some might easily dismiss microaggressions. Others could react angrily because of the way they process information. We've all seen people lash out in public—a scene that plays out in families, communities, and films. But sometimes, our anger is misplaced. We will react if we feel unloved or fearful that what we have is being taken away. Or it could just be one slight too many. The saying, "The straw that broke the camel's back", means just that. One can take only so many slights before they retreating or lashing out. The result can be catastrophic. Especially if one party wants revenge, which can be a natural instinct for some. When people seek revenge, they are consumed by anger. They can't think straight. They say and do things they might regret later. One hurt can lead to another. It doesn't solve the problem. It only makes matters worse. When cool heads prevail, we look beyond the heated moment; we determine what started the fight and what can be done to resolve differences.

On the topic of perceived slights, I'm reminded of a young married woman who was so angry with her husband's grandmother that she forbade her children and husband to see her. It happened one Christmas when she received scented drawer liners as a gift. She interpreted that present from her husband's grandmother as an insult to her housekeeping. She had been rejected by her own family over religious beliefs. Raised a Jehovah's Witness, she was cut off from her family when she married a man who wasn't. Was the gift from her husband's grandmother the straw that broke the camel's back? Likely still hurting over the loss of her own family ties, she refused to have anything to do with her husband's family.

None of us are perfect. People with the best intentions can trigger those who are easily hurt. We don't know what pain others carry. Or understand how a harsh tone or look can ruin a person's day. Sometimes, it can even cost us a relationship for life.

Others may find an avalanche of hurt is triggered by just one more hurtful incident. Like one man who found himself inexplicably angry at his mother's funeral. When the undertaker asked him to carry the urn with his mother's ashes to be placed beside his father's grave, the man balked. He didn't want to do it. Afterwards, he wondered why he had reacted so strongly. He loved his mother and had never shown anger towards her during her lifetime. Troubled, he sought help from a professional therapist; he wanted to understand his unexplained hard feelings. He discovered he'd been holding onto his anger for years, which he'd never expressed to his mother while she was alive. She hadn't been easy to deal with, so he hadn't shared his feelings for fear she would lash out at him. The therapist encouraged him to write her a letter—even though she was no longer alive—and say all the things he had wanted to say but felt he couldn't without serious repercussions. This simple act of writing down his feelings lightened the load he carried. He'd been harbouring regret and anger for too long. Writing the letter gave him peace. It allowed him to step back and deal with his anger yet embrace all the good times he'd experienced with his mother. After he finished the letter, he tore it up—putting his rage towards her to bed for good. He transitioned from anger to love within a short course of therapy and found the balance he needed to move forward.

Healthy behaviour means managing our hurts and our disappointments constructively. It means finding that balance, where we let those we care about know where we stand and what bothers us. It means communicating in a thoughtful and dignified way that is neither revengeful nor hurtful.

ADDICTION

Since I worked in a number of mental health settings, I encountered many who were hoping to overcome their addictions. But because addiction was not my area of expertise, I only worked with addicts for one or two sessions, just enough to give them hope and some new direction. The time was spent helping them connect with the resources that specialized in their type of addiction.

As Mark Twain once said, "Too much of anything is bad." People who are addicted can't seem to get enough of whatever they crave—drinking, drugging, overeating, gambling, gaming, sex, shopping. But when we look at what's happening today with so many of us addicted to our devices and social media, we can assume that addiction is more widespread than we think. Especially if we broaden the view. Considering the fact hundreds of millions need to check their phones habitually, it appears there is abundant evidence of our general vulnerability to addictive behaviour. While many of us manage to control our cravings, we need to be mindful oth when it affects our health, ability to work, and relationships, which is the case for those addicted to alcohol, other substances, and behaviours.

The question then, is not whether we are addicts, but rather, are we able to control our addictive tendencies or does the addiction control us?

Some say addicts don't have the willpower to abstain from alcohol or drugs; they say they're weak. Others argue that they've chosen to get impaired. The truth is more complicated than that.

We are a product of both nature and nurture. If you look at an addict's genogram, you'll likely see alcoholics or other addicts in their family tree. Now that we've learned more about the power of genetics, having addicts in your family tree suggests there is a possibility that some members will be vulnerable to an addiction that requires treatment if unchecked. And because of this, it will be more challenging for them to say "no" to substances or unhealthy activities that hurt them in the end.

In other words, we're not all wired the same way. But there is hope and available support for those who find it hard to stop abusing their bodies with substances that destroy their lives.

I recall working with a highly educated and well-known personality in British Columbia who had come to me for help with his alcoholism. He had tried Alcoholics Anonymous, but that support group hadn't helped. When we met, he wanted to enter a four-week intensive substance use program at Maple Ridge Treatment Centre, which is a good hour and a half from downtown Vancouver. I picked him up and drove him there. He brought a suitcase filled with clothes, toiletries, and books, along with a paper bag containing a mickey of whiskey. Though I wasn't an addiction counsellor, it was apparent he was on the fence about giving up alcohol. I wondered if

I was doing the right thing by allowing him to bring some alcohol for the ride. But maybe, I thought, he needed it to deal with his demons and face his fears of giving up the crutch that gave him so much relief from his daily pain. Being Indigenous, he had attended residential school, which we all know damaged so many and contributed to their drug dependency. Looking back, I suspect the paper bag holding the mickey (an old "friend") gave him some comfort during the car ride. Thankfully, the bottle stayed in the bag. When we arrived at the Maple Ridge Treatment Centre, the alcohol was confiscated before he was admitted. What's important to note here is that he chose to get treatment. Because addiction is a devil that's hard to kick to the curb, it takes incredible strength to choose a road of sobriety.

Free Will

To say, "I had no choice," is to avoid responsibility. It can be an easy out, but not a helpful one. In a sense, uttering *I had no choice* is a choice in itself. It's an excuse to blame someone else for our poor decisions. There is such a thing as free will. From the time we are infants, we make choices. Just watch a baby refuse to eat some food that their mother has put in front of them. If they try it and don't like the texture, smell, or taste, they will wrinkle their nose, tighten their mouth, and push the food away. Mother might not give up and use various cute tricks, but it will turn into an ordeal for both of them.

A Hard Road

As a therapist, I met many addicts, but as I mentioned, I wasn't a specialist, so I referred them to alcohol and drug counsellors after the first session or two. I understood the dynamics of what had led them to this dark place and then a cry for help, but I also knew it would be a hard road if they decided to stop drugging. In the throes of addiction, the addict won't admit they're abusing drugs or people in their life. Denial and lying are their ways of preserving their addiction and protecting themselves from criticism. They not only lie to others but also to themselves. They are so wrapped up in their fears of being found out they cannot see how their actions affect those who care about them.

Alcoholics Anonymous

Alcoholics Anonymous (A.A.), the worldwide organization for alcoholics hoping to conquer their addiction, tries to address this tendency to avoid responsibility by helping individuals through a twelve-step program. Each step helps the addict get closer to sobriety. Those who begin the A.A. program have accepted two things: they couldn't stop drinking alone, and they are an alcoholic. They agree to stop lying to themselves and those they love. In A.A., they find their community, people who understand what they're up against. They get the support they need to fight the battle against addiction.

A.A. is not a perfect model, but it recognizes some fundamental truths, which are underlined in *The Serenity Prayer*. Interestingly, the prayer has applications for everyone, even non-alcoholics.

The Serenity Prayer

God grant me the serenity
To accept the things I cannot change;
Courage to change the things I can.
And wisdom to know the difference.
Living one day at a time;
Enjoying one moment at a time;
Accepting hardships as the pathway to peace;
Taking, as He did, this sinful world
As it is, not as I would have it;
Trusting that He will make all things right
If I surrender to His Will;
So that I may be reasonably happy in this life
And supremely happy with Him
Forever and ever in the next.
Amen.

The first four lines of *The Serenity Prayer* are the ones that resonate the most with the general public: "God grant me the serenity to accept the things I cannot change, courage to change the things I can, and wisdom to know the difference." So much of life is out of our control but recognizing what we can control and change is critical to recovery. A.A. also asks members to surrender to a higher power, which can be problematic for those who don't believe in God. However, the intention behind this rule is good. It's meant to help members know they are not alone and that there is a higher being they can count on for support.

The pull of drugs is hard to overcome. Besides genetics, your environment is also a factor: family, friends, peers, school, workplace, culture, religion, and community.

In a biographical fiction trilogy based on my grandmother's life, *Lukia's Family Saga,* I wrote about one of my uncles, who became an alcoholic and led a tragic life because of it. He grew up in a family that had a habit of having a shot with their meal after a hard day of work on the farm. In Ukrainian culture, family and friends enjoy alcohol with their food (yes, we socialize like the Italians and French). Laughter and song accompany whiskey, wine, or shots of vodka. However, during my uncle's formative years, there was little attention given to alcohol use as a problem. They were more concerned with survival in a country that always seemed to be at war. Sure, there would be the village drunk, but many drank themselves into oblivion to soothe themselves and dull the pain of their lives. My uncle's father and grandfather drank heavily too. Were they alcoholics? I don't know, but I hazard a guess they were. His grandfather, a lumber contractor, lost all his money through both his drunken generosity and poor decisions. So, my uncle was not only vulnerable to addiction because of his environment—all the drinking at the family table—but also his inherited genes. His drinking problem carried over onto Canadian soil when my uncle and his family left Ukraine to immigrate in 1929. He never got the help he needed. A.A. didn't start until the mid 1930s, and that was in the USA. It would take another eight to ten years before the organization established a foothold in Canadian cities. I expect rural areas had to wait even longer.

Positive Addiction

Dr. William Glasser, an American psychiatrist, wrote a book called *Positive Addiction.* He made the case that addicts can choose a positive addiction like running. They can run until their beta-endorphins (happy hormones) kick in, which takes about twenty minutes. Creative hobbies, continuous learning, and other forms of regular exercise are also good choices. We see positive addiction in the population. Playing Wordle, the New York Times word game became popular world-wide. Other word games or card games, like Solitaire, serve a similar purpose. Others may take up knitting, crocheting, or whittling as ways to relax their mind. Though time-consuming, these are healthier choices. They don't affect our mental and physical health the way alcohol and other substances do. Quite the opposite. These activities stimulate our mind in a good way.

Drugs may numb the pain of a toxic marriage, lost connections, family trauma, a horrible job, and post-traumatic stress, but their impact is horrendous. Still, many have overcome their addiction. There are countless stories of people who have gone dry; they gave up the substances that destroyed them and chose another way to lift their spirits. They used services available to them for healing. They likely had the support of a close friend, a loving family member, or a caring therapist. But ultimately, the choice was theirs.

One Novel Solution

One novel solution to addiction was shown on the CBS program *60 Minutes* in January 2024. Gerod Buckhalter, a young American who used to be a promising football player, told his story about getting hooked on heavy-duty painkillers to cope with a shoulder injury. An addict of opiates for eighteen years, he had gone through a vicious cycle of drugging, attempting suicide, and rotating through the revolving doors of treatment centres. But when neurosurgeon Dr. Ali Rezai used focused ultrasound to alter the spot in Buckhalter's brain that kept urging him to use drugs, he became a changed man. No longer did he crave painkillers or illicit hard drugs (like heroin).

In desperation, Buckhalter had volunteered to be a guinea pig for Dr. Rezai's new study. Not everyone has the dramatic opportunity to work with a world-renowned neurosurgeon as part of their treatment. But this special treatment offers addicts new hope. There is growing support for those who find it hard to control their urges because of inherited genetics or challenges in their upbringing. Still, many have recovered from addiction in time-tested ways. In Buckhalter's case, signing up for the experiment was an option to seek treatment. But as we've discussed, it's not always a simple choice.

CULTIVATING

REALITY UNDERLINED

While working at the Child Guidance Clinic, I had the good fortune to hear Dr. William Glasser speak about reality therapy, a method of psychotherapy he'd developed in the mid-1960s. He arrived in Winnipeg after a big snowstorm had paralyzed the city for a day or two. His speech had been delayed because driving was slow and treacherous. When he finally got to the podium, he said roughly the following: "On my way to speak to you, I saw several motorists stuck in the snow. And what were they doing to get out of the snow? They were spinning their wheels, and their tires were getting them in deeper. Did they get out of their cars and say to themselves: *This isn't working*? *Maybe I should try something different?* No, they didn't do that. Instead, they got back in their car and continued doing the same thing. They pressed their foot on the gas pedal, only harder."

Glasser used that analogy to illustrate how we do the same thing in life. We see this repetitive behaviour in families. A parent who disciplines their child by yelling will yell even harder when they misbehave again. In response, the child either becomes deaf to all that yelling—tuning their parent out—or digs their heels in and misbehaves even more. For many, they crave the attention, even if it's negative.

This repetitive pattern serves no one.

Dr. Glasser went on to say that *"if what we're doing isn't getting us what we want, then we need to change what we're doing."* He emphasized that we can't control anyone's behaviour, but we can control our own. If we change what we're doing, the other party will not be able to respond in the same way. It'll break the pattern and make room for a healthier one. It could mean asserting ourselves differently, walking away, reacting calmly, or changing our words. The list of possibilities is endless. Initially, changing our behaviour will feel odd, but in time it too will feel normal.

Dr. Glasser's point bears repeating: "If what we're doing isn't getting us what we want, then we should change what we're doing." It's a lesson I've long remembered. It's hard to put into practice because we develop habits that are hard to break as adults. Change like this is hard, but it pays enormous dividends.

Even in our gardens.

Several years back, I bought a hydrangea plant that was failing. The price was so low I couldn't resist. I knew nothing about this shrub but was up for the challenge. At first, it wasn't happy even though I tried everything. The plant's foliage—scorched and dry leaves—showed it was struggling, so I moved it to a less sunny location by the garage. Though it was on the south side of the house, the garage provided the plant with shade and shelter from the scorching summer sun at midday. It is now thriving. Again, I tried something different rather than doing more of the same. Human relationships are more complicated, but it still holds true, that a different approach can yield different results.

What follows are a few examples of challenging relationships. Glasser's ideas can make a difference.

The Family Scapegoat

When someone is labelled as the scapegoat in the family, it is difficult for them to cultivate change and get out of that role because other family members will unconsciously conspire against them no matter what they do. It's an adopted pattern that's hard to change. The ongoing pattern of blame dogs the individual.

However, those labelled as scapegoats may have spirited personalities or engage in behaviour that frustrates other family members. Still, none are as helpless as we may think. There are ways for everyone in a family grouping to grow and learn from those who stand out in one way or another.

If you have someone in your family who is challenging—quarrelsome, shifts the truth, avoids taking responsibility, or blames others for the problems in their life—you can at least get some distance and arrive at a point where you accept what is and don't worry about changing the status quo. You can make decisions based on your future. Perhaps you can temper your involvement, see them less, or separate altogether. Changing what you've been doing is bound to stop you from going in circles. The act of distancing yourself may not change the dynamic of the relationship, but it can bring some peace to your life.

Living with an Abuser

Living with someone mentally ill and/or abusive can be an intolerable situation. We can accept that anyone who's a victim of abuse and neglect has a right to fight back. But here's the problem: sometimes, the difficult personality is too powerful. If the person is in a position of power, such as in a parent-child or spousal relationship in which they are the sole support, they have a hold on others financially, physically, and emotionally. They may use intimidation and emotional abuse or withhold money to gain power and control.

This was the case for a young mother who called me and asked for help to deal with her abusive husband. They had argued soon after their first child was born, and he had hit her repeatedly with a phone receiver while she was lying in bed with their baby. She wanted help with their relationship. She'd called the police and told her husband she was leaving. Unfortunately, when the police arrived, she had a change of heart. She forgave him. Forgiveness is all well and good, but if the perpetrator of the abuse has not accepted that they were at fault and shown a willingness to change, all forgiveness does is give the abuser a break before the cycle of abuse continues again.

Shortly after the incident involving the police, she came in to see me. Though she had dropped the charges and forgiven him, he refused to come in for counselling. Still, she felt he had changed. She said she loved him and that he truly knew he had to reform this time. He had apologized, brought her flowers, and vowed not to hit her again. This is a familiar pattern for abusers in domestic violence cases. An argument that triggers physical and emotional abuse is followed by an apology and a promise not to do it again. It may be a good start for the abuser to express remorse, but it's not nearly enough. Not when there's been an unhealthy pattern of rage and escalation. Not when those they profess to love get hurt.

Unless the abuser takes responsibility for their actions and undergoes treatment for anger management, nothing will change. The victim can't control the abuser's behaviour; only the abuser can. However, the victimcan stop the vicious cycle of abuse by being assertive from the start. Demanding the abuser go for help before their behaviour falls into a threatening and dangerous pattern. There is no shortage of media coverage about women running for their lives from former partners. Out of both fear and love, they had given their partners one chance after another to no avail.

The only recourse for people being abused is to leave if they want to remain safe. But as I observed in my practice, the abused can be easily swayed to stay in the relationship when their partner showers them with terms of endearment and gives them flowers or an apology. Perhaps this is why so many people stay with their abusers. Love certainly has something to do with it, but often, they feel they have no choice. They may have no family to turn to, no other place to live, and no money to carry them through until they can get on their feet. They may also worry about judgement; they may feel some shame about their situation. They may even believe the abuser who says the out-of-control situation is their fault.

Author Stephanie Land captured this predicament in her 2019 memoir *Maid,* which was adapted into a hit Netflix series of the same name. The book depicts her desperate attempt to leave her physically abusive husband. He was fine when he wasn't drinking, but when he did, he turned into a threatening and violent monster.

There are countless examples of women who can't outrun their abusers. And yet, their choice to stay is perilous. Women need to leave before they and/or their children get hurt. Fortunately, many find help in transition houses and safe homes—temporary housing for battered women. Here, they get counselling and support to figure out how to manage on their own. Many need police protection, even when they have a restraining order. In hindsight, many wish they had made a different choice. In the heat of passion, they had ignored the telltale signs of an abuser: extreme jealousy, possessiveness, mood swings, controlling behaviour, and threats.

Abusers often have a history of child abuse. But many become abusive only when under the influence of drugs and alcohol. It changes how they feel and act. For those who don't wrestle with an addictive personality, a few glasses of wine or pints of beer with friends is simply a way to relax. But it can be a slippery slope for those with little impulse control.

The Problem with Labels

G ardeners like labels; it helps them understand what a plant needs for optimum growth—how deep to plant seeds and vegetation, whether they like sun or shade or a bit of both, and what soil conditions they prefer.

Healthcare professionals in various fields also assign labels to patients based on the behaviour they're presenting. But unlike the precise instructions we get from seed packets and gardening manuals, the labels for humans sometimes fit and sometimes they don't. The wrong label can throw people onto a path that doesn't serve them; in fact, it can even harm them.

Labelling the Young

In the school system, there are always students who take up an inordinate amount of a teacher's time. Like plants in a garden, some need more tending than others. Labelling some kids as rebellious or withdrawn doesn't solve the problem. Their situations are more complex in today's schools where resources are few. In fact, labelling may exacerbate an already challenging classroom dynamic that includes bullying and other forms of peer mistreatment. At best, children who require extra attention should be assessed holistically to prevent further harm. Though they present a challenge to the adults who care for them, they often have unique qualities that could enrich their classmates' experience, if given half a chance.

If the teacher is fortunate to have a social worker to call on, they will assess the child's situation at home to see whether a problem there is affecting the student's academic performance and classroom behaviour. They'll also consider the child's personality and innate abilities. But because the mind is so complex, inappropriate labels are not that uncommon.

The feature film, *Gifted,* shows a great example of how a teacher's sensitive handling of a new and socially awkward young student pays dividends. Considered a mathematical genius at seven, Mary was accustomed to speaking out of turn and disrupting the class. On one occasion, she reacted violently when she saw an older student bully a young boy in her classroom. She broke the older student's nose. Rather than punish her in traditional ways, the teacher and principal—while still underlining the gravity of what she had done—taught her the importance of restraint when provoked and how to behave appropriately in the classroom. Mary also had to reassure her classmates she was not to be feared. Afterwards, there's a lovely scene where Mary asks the teacher for permission to speak. And when she does, she praises the young boy's art project that had been destroyed by the bully. There's applause and smiles all around, especially from the boy who was bullied.

For three years, I worked as a family counsellor at the Children's Foundation in Vancouver, which provides specialized treatment to children with complex challenges. They had been placed there by the Ministry of Human Resources because all parties involved—social workers, school personnel, and parents—didn't know how to help them. These children were troublesome at school and at home. Childcare counsellors—who managed the treatment of the children at the Children's Foundation—asked me to see the family of one eight-year-old boy because he continued to be defiant, even in the residential children's treatment program. The counsellors were struggling how to teach him to cooperate and follow the rules. Because I had previously worked in a multidisciplinary team—with a psychiatrist, a psychologist, a social worker, a reading clinician, and a speech and hearing therapist—at the Child Guidance Clinic in Winnipeg, I picked up on the fact that the boy was not cooperating because he didn't understand what was being asked of him. I recommended a referral to an audiologist for some hearing tests, which, sure enough, revealed the boy had an auditory processing disorder (APD). He could not process what was being asked of him. Once this problem was identified, the audiologist informed the staff and the family of how to approach the boy. Instead of being labelled defiant, he was recognized as a child with a hearing challenge.

This story is only one example of how we can miss the mark with incorrect labels. Again, every child is unique and needs to be understood within their environment. We must consider their persreonality traits and how they help or hinder them.

Labelling in Mental Health

It's worthwhile to note that caregivers, while trying to do their best, are challenged when dealing with people who have an illness that affects their minds. Problems with labels are not uncommon in mental health. Even with a diagnostic manual, many people are misdiagnosed.

I recall coming across a psychiatric file of a patient diagnosed with schizophrenia one month and manic-depressive illness (now known as bipolar disorder) the next. The mind is so complex that it's often difficult to determine what disorder patients are sufferin from.

Recently, another case of misdiagnosis came to light when the husband of a friend was mislabeled as 'a danger to himself and others' and admitted for Tertiary Psychiatric Care at Royal Jubilee Hospital in Victoria, British Columbia. This is the story of what happened in his wife's words:

This incident happened fourteen years after my husband was diagnosed with Alzheimer's disease. He was attending a daycare program three mornings a week. The manager called one afternoon to explain there had been an incident and asked if I could pick Bill up. She said he had threatened to choke a worker during a bathroom break, but he hadn't hurt or touched her. However, she had been badly frightened. Following the incident, the manager asked Bill what had happened. He said he didn't know; he'd just felt like he'd wanted to kill someone. The manager then asked him if he wanted to have lunch with the other clients at the daycare; he said yes, ate lunch, then put on his jacket to go home. That's when she called me.

My daughter was home and heard my conversation with the manager. She said it was a serious threat, and her dad needed to go to the ER.

In Emergency, I explained what was relayed to me by daycare and said emphatically that Bill had never hurt me or anyone else. Though Bill lay calmly on the stretcher beside me, I was told by the Liaison Nurse that if I didn't admit him and agree to voluntary Tertiary Psychiatric Care, Bill would never get a bed in a long-term care facility in our community.

I went home for supper and returned later to find Bill tied to a stretcher and drugged under the glaring lights in the hallway. He was twisting in pain, trying to relieve the pressure on his back and free himself from the restraints.

I went looking for a nurse. When I found one, she said, "He became combative." No other explanation was given.

Though restrained and drugged, Bill was fully aware of what was happening to him. The psychiatrist told the Charge Nurse that Bill would lose all his strength if he continued to be restrained like that. But because he had thoroughly scared her, she wanted him to remain restrained. There was no thought given to how he was feeling, nor how these restraints were being interpreted by others. It's well to note that if a patient is restrained like that, other hospital staff, including security, believe they are dangerous.

I went to our GP's office and begged him to order staff to remove the restraints entirely. The second time, I demanded it. Then, Bill was free to at least walk around his room, which was locked from the outside, so he could not get out. For the next few weeks, I could see that

Bill was becoming more and more frustrated. Some of the staff didn't seem to realize the drugs were impairing his ability to hear and follow directions. Over time, he began to react by pushing some staff out of his personal space when they attempted to provide personal care. Then, I asserted myself more fully and started taking him home for several hours a day. He fully cooperated with me no matter what I did for him.

One Saturday morning, seven weeks after he was hospitalized, Bill's nurse called me at ten o'clock to report that she could not get near him to provide personal care. "Can you come?" she said. He had apparently been ramped up and resistant to care all morning.

When I arrived, I immediately entered Bill's room and took his hand to take him to the bathroom. He pushed me away. I realized I'd moved too fast, stepped back, and asked if he wanted me to help him get cleaned up. He said yes. The bathroom was tiny, only room for Bill to stand backwards to the toilet and for me to stand sideways in the doorway beside him. Again, I spoke to him gently, and he agreed to let me help him. I took him home that afternoon and again the following day. But a day later, when we went to leave, the Director of Nurses blocked the doorway. "You can't take him out," she said. I disagreed and cited the fact I had a legal representation agreement. She asked, "Did Bill punch, hit, and kick you?"

I was dumbfounded. "No, of course not."

She said, "I have witnesses."

Stunned, I soon realized she must have been talking about Saturday. "I moved too fast at first" I said, "and Bill pushed me. That's all he did. I'll show you." I then demonstrated.

Our GP arrived not long after and blocked the door. "I can't allow you to take him out," he said. "I'm certifying him as 'a danger to himself and others.'

I completely lost it! I shouted that I had a legal representation agreement, and he could not stop me. By now, I was sobbing loudly. "Please don't do this" I said. "He's never hurt anyone!" I told him exactly what happened, but he wasn't listening. He was busy texting the psychiatrist in Comox, who would have to second the certification for it to be enforced.

That afternoon, Bill was moved to the Psychiatric Unit at Comox Valley Hospital. Three weeks later, he was admitted for Tertiary Psychiatric Care at Royal Jubilee Hospital in Victoria. Over the next seven months, I spent four days a week in Bill's ward for four to ten hours each day. Eventually, the ward staff left Bill's personal care mostly to me. For all that time, I fought to free my husband. In the end, I hired a lawyer to help me. Two days and two telephone conferences later, I was finally able to bring Bill home. He had spent nine months confined, drugged, and given ECT treatments I had not authorized—ECT being the single thing I still had the legal authority to accept or deny. He had declined exponentially in every way. But he spent his last months at home. If I had it to do again, I would not agree to Bill being hospitalized in the first place.

Bill's story is a cautionary tale. He had said, "I just felt like I wanted to kill someone." This was enough to set the psychiatric wheels in motion. Who hasn't felt rage at times? Who hasn't said words in the heat of the moment that they would never act upon?

Suffering from Alzheimer's, the poor man needed support, understanding, and gentle care. Instead, he was mislabeled as dangerous, and well-meaning caregivers saw nothing else from that point on. Today, we know that Alzheimer's can affect emotions. The elderly suffering from this affliction can become easily confused and, as a result, extremely angry. In this situation, a misdiagnosis led to considerable damage not only to the individual but also to his family.

Labelling the Elderly

The elderly are especially vulnerable. With their physical and mental faculties deteriorating, they find all too often their complaints easily dismissed or misdiagnosed. Some years ago, the impact of mislabeling hit home when my mother was hospitalized for a heart condition while I was visiting her in Winnipeg. She needed a pacemaker. The operation went well, but just when she was about to be discharged, she developed gout, which delayed her release. At the time, Grace Hospital had a C. difficile outbreak in her ward; it was so bad that several patients died. Then, Mom contracted that serious bacterial infection. My one-week visit turned into two months when my mother ended up in isolation. To see her, I had to gown up and don latex gloves.

One morning, I found her on the commode by her bed. She yelled, "Help me, help me! Will somebody help me?" I don't know how long she had been yelling. Her eyes bulged, and she kept snapping her head back towards the door. I assume she was hoping a nurse would come. I barely recognized my mother. She wasn't the wild-eyed type, nor was she a difficult woman. I was also surprised none of the staff came running. After I calmed my mother down, I went to the nurse in charge and asked what medications she was on. The nurse told me Dilaudid had been prescribed the day before. She was now taking it, besides a potassium supplement, antibiotics and meds for high blood pressure, an overactive bladder, arthritis, and Parkinson's. I immediately looked up Dilaudid and learned it's a narcotic given for moderate-to-severe pain; it can have serious side effects, especially for a woman in her nineties.

It was then I discovered that one nurse had labeled Mom as difficult and demanding. To give the staff the benefit of the doubt, the doctor had prescribed Dilaudid to calm her. I found that curious as I had been visiting her for weeks and had heard no complaints from her about any pain. I don't know what went on at night, but the woman I saw that day was not the mother I knew. As her advocate—every patient should have one—I asked the doctor to please take her off the narcotic. When he did, my mother returned to her normal self.

I know many doctors believe in a holistic approach to health problems. It's essential to monitor a patient's medication closely for detrimental side effects, as each person's health profile is unique. This can be a tall order, given the global shortage of doctors. Our healthcare professionals are often busy with huge patient loads. It's difficult for them to keep track of each patient's needs. If no follow-up appointment is booked, the onus is on the patient to call back and ensure they get the attention they need.

Like healthcare professionals, we can rush to judgment. We all want to solve a problem. We feel some progress when we think we know what we're dealing with. However, we need to be cautious about labeling our family members and other people who are important to us. Coming up with the wrong label can lead them down a road that doesn't help anyone.

CHOICES

We make choices from the time we are born. Our instincts kick in immediately. We cry because of discomfort, hunger, or fatigue. But we quickly notice those around us and how they can meet our needs. As mentioned earlier, we don't stay down when we fall during our attempts to walk. We get up and try again. Our curiosity takes us places. We choose what toy to play with, what food to put in our mouths, and what to push away. Even as babies, we figure out how to get what we want. When we grow up into adults, we have even more choices everywhere we turn: the jobs we take, the company we keep, the places we live, and the roads we travel.

Just as we choose what we put in our gardens, we also decide how we live our lives. Many of us plod along with routines dictated by work, family, and society, giving little thought to how else we can manage and spend our time. And yet, every new year, many of us make resolutions and vow to do something different. We almost invariably break these resolutions, not because we're fickle or weak. It's often because we haven't stepped back to assess what we're doing to reinforce unhealthy behaviour, and what we need to do differently to get closer to what we want.

Many years ago, I read the lovely little book *On Choosing with a Quiet Mind* by Ray H. Woollam. He describes it as "a Zen-like view of work and the workplace." At the start of each chapter, he wrote, "*You can have all the fairies you like in your back garden, just as long as you know that you put them there.*"

Woollam uses examples from his workplace to illustrate his point. He shows readers how people often say, "I had no choice," when explaining why they're doing what they're doing. They don't realize they made the decision. We always have a choice.

Life's Direction

One of the most significant decisions we make in life has to do with work. What occupation should we pursue? What education and training will put us on the career path of our dreams? It's not an easy choice. Time, money, and opportunity are all factors in this decision.

The bestseller *What Color Is Your Parachute* gives the reader exercises to help them decide what direction to take in life. It's a book I've recommended to many who expressed unhappiness with their work and were at a loss about what to do next. They had chosen a line of work that wasn't satisfying. They felt stuck in their jobs. They weren't sure if they had the skills, experience, or time to consider other options. The problem had reared its ugly head because they were working in a toxic work environment where their superior or colleagues gave them grief and caused them stress. Working under such circumstances was affecting their mental and physical health.

Rather than divulge any of my clients' journeys, I'll share my own. I've danced around a lot, more so than most. I had many questions as to what occupation would fit my interests, perhaps because I have both a well-developed right brain (the creative half) and well-developed left brain (the analytical half). Some aspects of both the artistic and scientific fields appealed to me. Prior to this search, I had worked in many occupations. In fact, I often joke that I'm a Jill of all trades. That varied experience has given me interesting material for my writing, as I've held both blue-collar and white-collar jobs, and I'm all the richer for it. But there was a point when I wondered what I should do next. I wasn't sure that I was in the right field.

What Color Is Your Parachute helped me reflect on my interests, skill set, education, and the kind of work I'd find enjoyable. The exercises steered me in the right direction.

But I also understand that many people don't have the luxury of quitting or taking a break from work to consider other possibilities. After all, there are bills to pay. But surely, an hour can be found here and there after work a few times each week to begin exploring two crucial questions: *what else is out there,* and *what else am I suited for?* There's a reason *What Color Is Your Parachute* remains a bestseller a half-century later. Questioning your line of work is common, especially if you've fallen into your occupation without considerable thought. If you're unhappy with what you're doing to support yourself, take the time to explore other options. You owe it to yourself.

It's not surprising that countless workers changed jobs during and after the COVID pandemic. Though many worked (remotely) during this period, they had time to consider their occupation and what else was out there. Many realized they enjoyed working from home and did not want to go back to spending long hours commuting. Both employers and employees found that productivity increased. Some worked out a new arrangement with their employer, others left for new horizons. Many managers questioned the high cost of maintaining offices downtown in urban centres, especially when their workers preferred to work from home. As for those in the healthcare field who had to work during this trying time, they, too, considered their options when the pressures at work eased. Many also found that with masks and better hygiene, they were actually healthier. Fewer colds and less flu. That is, if they didn't get COVID.

A new world problem is managing all the choices we have today. Everything is at our fingertips, for those who can afford them. In our neighbourhoods, there is often a wide range of restaurants with varied menus, and community centres packed with activities for all ages. Streaming services offer so many programming choices. And then, there are our devices, giving us access to the news, social media, and podcasts for stimulating conversations.

Fear of Missing Out

And along with these choices comes FOMO—the fear of missing out. If we're at all curious, we're constantly juggling the demands we put on ourselves. There's always somewhere to go, something to do, and someone to see for those with friends and money. This fear propels many to overbook their days, leaving little time for rest and relaxation. It's akin to a hamster on a wheel, going round and round and not getting anywhere. No time to deal with the essentials. It can be overwhelming, especially if these self-imposed demands get in the way of a proper night's rest and a healthy, balanced diet. Fatigue and frustration follow.

If you are always tired, that's a clue you're doing too much. If your home is disorganized and you're not eating properly, that's another hint. Returning to Maslow's Hierarchy of Needs, we must take care of the basics to feel right with the world. Again, when you're thinking of choices, what are your priorities? What are your needs? Are you meeting them? Or are they being shunted to one side because you can't resist the temptation to check out highlight reels on social media? It's too easy to buy into the illusion that everyone else is living their best life.

Slowing down helps. Establishing a routine gives your body clock some much-needed rhythm—like regular meals and seven to eight hours of sleep every night. It's more difficult for those with young children. Still, we have choices. We all have them. It's up to you to decide how you want to live your life.

ACCEPTING DIFFERENCES

This chapter is not about accepting differences in society, although it is a worthy topic. It's more about accepting differences in our immediate circle of family and friends.

Each person grows up in a family with unique communication patterns. Everything from values to political views and religious beliefs may differ from one household to the next. It's common and natural that when couples get together, each partner tries to get the other to think like them. We can see why this approach can lead to conflict. Without taking the time to get to know our other half, we can easily get frustrated when they disagree with us. And yet, we're attracted to opposites, who we hope share our values and interests.

As the name suggests, the bestselling book *Men Are from Mars, Women Are from Venus* by John Gray speaks to the differences between men and women. Conflict between the two sexes is so universal that comedians like to joke about problems in their relationships and not understanding their mates. They give familiar examples to the audience, who respond with applause and resounding peals of laughter.

Rather than trying to convince your spouse to think the same way you do, you're more likely to gain ground by stepping back and accepting your differences. You may not agree with their viewpoint or way of doing things, but love and respect go a long way toward resolving conflict. You can then meet in the middle or accept your partner's reasoning. They may do the same.

There are many differences to explore with a life partner. You have each gone through a unique set of early life experiences. By the time you meet, there is much to consider. Was your family lower, middle, or upper class? Did you speak any other language besides English in your home? Were there important customs and traditions you would want to continue? What role did the women in your family assume? Was there equality when it came to household chores? Who was the breadwinner? Who took care of money? How were financial decisions made? Were you an only child? Or did you grow up in a home with a large, rambunctious family where disputes, debates, and sibling rivalry were seen as normal? Did the head of the household spout nonsense like 'My way or the highway!' When you broke the rules, were you scolded, beaten, sent to your room, or faced with some other response? What are your thoughts on having children or child-rearing? Did your family encourage you to share your feelings, or did you learn to hide your worries and joys? Were there family secrets? If so, how did they affect you? How did you know right from wrong? And how was that different from what your partner learned? What about your likes and dislikes? Are you an omnivore, carnivore, pescatarian, vegan, or vegetarian? Are you active in sports or a couch potato? Is faith important to you? Do you appreciate art, theatre, and film or would you rather stay home and read or play video games? Are you a loner, or do you love to socialize? Do you like to travel or stay at home?

When we mate, it's widely expected that there will be differences, but falling in love with someone who thinks differently than us on all fronts does not bode well for the future. It doesn't mean the relationship is doomed. Hard work, patience, understanding, compromise, and communication will be necessary to overcome the negative emotions that accompany marked differences.

We have all heard cultural stories about parents who wring their hands when their child falls in love with someone from a different class, race, or religion. Perhaps it's happened in your family. Though some of us criticize those who can't accept change or differences, it is understandable to worry about your child meeting someone from another race. We are comfortable with what we know, not so much with what we don't. Our parents may fear that old traditions and customs will be eroded or lost. But the world has become one global community, as illustrated in the shows and films we see and the stories we read. Today's audiences are ready to accept the diversity around us.

In short, navigating differences can stimulate a relationship, but one too many might be a bridge too far. We see that conundrum in Nature. Nature shows that various plants can grow side by side in harmony, like trees in a forest, but some cannot. It all depends on their individual needs.

Managing conflict and other threats to marital unity is the key to a happy marriage. Although opposites attract, it's common for a couple to see a therapist to complain about their spouse who thinks differently and wants different things in life. They often spend the early years of their marriage or marriage-like relationship trying to get their partner to adopt their way of thinking. It's difficult to see the other person's point of view when you're so stuck in your own.

One couple came to see me for marital counselling because they couldn't agree on how they wanted to spend their time after work hours. It was a May-December romance. It was a second marriage for the husband; he was a few decades older than his wife. He wanted to stay home and tend to the rhododendrons in his garden; she wanted to go out for dinner and then dance in a club. I'm not sure what drew this couple together, but their vast age difference led to inherent differences in how they wanted to spend their leisure time. This source of conflict was driving them apart. They'd grown up in different periods of history. And the husband brought the ghost of his former wife and their two children into his second marriage. Again, marked differences can be exciting to manage, but sometimes it becomes a chasm too difficult to cross.

With over 40 per cent of first marriages breaking up today, many are understandably taking their time to marry and raise kids. If you grew up in a broken home, you are more likely to get a divorce. Your marriage doesn't have to end this way, but having parents who called it quits may make you work harder to save your own union or give you a reason to leave.

There is no such thing as perfection in a relationship. The 'happily ever after' ending in Disney films and other Hollywood movies is a lovely concept, but it simplifies the love that binds two people together. It takes work to understand, appreciate, and value another person's views on life. We may not agree with each other, but respect for differences goes a long way.

My Story

I was in my first year of the Master of Social Work program at the University of Manitoba when I read a chapter called "Accepting Differences" in Virginia Satir's book *Conjoint Marital Therapy*. Equipped with some knowledge of marital behaviour, I thought I was becoming an authority. I even criticized my mother and father to their faces. I told them they needed to change their relationship. It would've been more acceptable for me to give criticism if they had asked me for help, but they hadn't complained about each other. In fact, they actually had a pretty good marriage. They never raised their voices, and together, they worked hard to care for me and my grandmother, who lived with us. If there was a disagreement they couldn't sort out in the moment, my father would go into the garage and tinker with his car. In turn, my mother would hoe the garden for hours as if every weed needed to be removed before she could return to the house. Did they talk about their argument later? I don't know. I'm assuming they must've, as I experienced harmony at home. Often, I heard them giggling in bed after dark. Their decision to leave a heated scene meant they were putting their disagreement on hold or perhaps burying it, at least for a little while. Perhaps they understood it was an excellent way to get some perspective, cool down, and avoid reacting when emotions are high. They had their own way of keeping peace in their relationship, and I should have respected that.

Now that I've reached their age, I reflect on my audacity with fresh eyes. I realize how young and uninformed I was. Their way of communicating as a couple may not have been my way, but it worked for them. And on further reflection, I have to give them credit for keeping the lid on a boiling kettle. The small steam they let out in the garage and the garden served them well. They were wonderful parents, and I'm grateful for their love and guidance.

I've been married to the love of my life for sixty-two years. I feel lucky to have weathered a few marital storms and grown old with Robert. Was it perfect? No. But he was perfect for me. We learned from each other. It took time and work. As we've aged, additional problems have emerged: fatigue and growing physical challenges. Thankfully, we are better equipped now to deal with anything that comes up.

Different Perceptions

It seems humans have had difficulty accepting people with different opinions and outlooks on life since time immemorial. In the heat of the moment, emotions flare and spill over, igniting others to react in kind. Accepting differences means practicing active listening and admitting that our way isn't the only way. It's also acknowledging the fact we don't all hear and see alike. We can have a conversation and come away with a different memory from the person we've engaged with. This is especially true when emotions are high.

When I was a psychotherapist, I would say to a couple in conflict, "You each have your own truth. Though you were in the same room, you have different perceptions of what happened. You remember some details but can't recall others. You each chose to focus on certain things; you came out of it with different memories. And each of you is processing what occurred through your history and how you view the world."

A good therapist will translate and help both partners understand how their communication went off the rails.

Learning from Nature

I live in constant amazement at the unique characteristics of each plant. Each flower's size, shape, petals, and scent distinguishes it from another. We marvel at their beauty and their strength. We have no trouble accepting variety in a garden, but we struggle to find common ground in life, as seen in the growing tension between many countries.

One only needs to look at the events leading up to the presidential election in the United States—the polarizing political divide and the ugly discourse online—to see the challenges many face in accepting differences. Some people have no qualms hiding behind their anonymous social media profiles to hurl invective at others. And with few people verifying their posts for slander or misinformation, the social media platform X has become an ugly place.

It's too bad we can't learn from Nature. Yes, there are predators. Living things don't always get along, but plants and animals seem to live in more harmony than humans.

SEEDING

DEFINING THE RELATIONSHIP

When we plan our garden, we look at the height, colour, and size of plants in relation to trees and one another. We look for what will fit our idea of a sublime landscape with beautiful composition and complementary vegetation. Similarly, we are attracted to those who complement us in personal relationships.

Relationships are defined by the people in them. Boss-employee, parent-child, sibling-sibling, partner-partner, husband-wife, and so on. How, what, and when we communicate can make or break a relationship.

During the building of any relationship, rules are set—often unspoken. If both parties agree on the rules, the relationship blossoms. But if they disagree and show disrespect through their words or behaviour, friction can tear away at the love that brought them together.

Changing Times

What we expect from our marital and family relationships has evolved. Today, marriage is a legally and socially sanctioned union in many countries, where people have the freedom to choose who they want to spend their life with, regardless of sexual orientation and religion.

But many people in other parts of the world aren't so lucky. Israel, Jordan, Lebanon, and Indonesia prohibit interfaith marriage. India, Italy, Japan, South Korea, and the Czech Republic still have not moved to legalize same-sex marriage. Other countries also continue to push for a traditional marriage between a man and a woman. Still, times have changed dramatically in the 21st century. The Netherlands made history when it legally recognized the first same-sex marriage in 2001. Since then, many countries—such as Canada, the United Kingdom, Ireland, and the United States—have followed suit. Taiwan became the first country in Asia to legalize same-sex marriage in 2019. It's also now legal in Thailand, Greece, Nepal, and Liechtenstein, as of 2024. The acronym LGBT has expanded to LGBTQ2S+ to represent lesbian, gay, bisexual, transgender, queer or questioning, and two-spirit identities. Though sexuality in all its forms is no longer taboo in Western society, many do not accept it.

I grew up in the 1950s when I only knew two genders—male and female. It was a simpler time. The main idea of gender identity has become confusing for many. Some are confused about the use of 'they' and 'them' to denote non-binary sex. Non-binary is an umbrella term for people who don't strictly identify as male or female. Those who find it hard to accept these new definitions look back fondly at the gender conceptions of their youth. But those times were full of denial and ignorance. Just because you put a blindfold on, it doesn't mean the view in front is gone.

In short, people's varied sexual responses are now out in the open, even though it's nothing new. One only needs to look at ancient art to see intimate images of various couples other than heterosexual. It's the same in Nature, where same-sex couplings are found in many mammals.

Unfortunately, there's been considerable backlash from those who cannot accept anything other than heterosexual unions. What makes us uncomfortable is sure to cause a stir, but there's no question that times have changed. And along with that, our expectations. But no matter how much churches, social groups, and different faiths protest against this sexual revolution, it's here to stay. With social media and the power of the internet, young people today grow up with more knowledge of what's possible for them in every way. Though the challenges are different today, young people are doing what they've always done—they test their boundaries. They explore their surroundings, break away from their parents, and find their own path. It's an emotional time. This is where parents and caregivers come in; they need to listen, consider their child's age and stage of development, and provide love and understanding. Adolescents also have to contend with raging hormones as they navigate life. Without community and family support, they might make rash decisions, which can affect them for years and maybe even decades to come.

As mentioned earlier, we can't think logically when we're emotionally upset. Despite their brave face, our youth need guidance. Now more than ever. Social media is seductive, especially for the young, whose eyes are fixed on their devices 24/7. There is no shortage of stories about parents dealing with tantrums because they've limited their children's time on their phones or taken them away. Every generation has its challenges.

Youth and the COVID Pandemic

Stories of youth suffering from anxiety and depression abound, some of which were brought on by unexpected lockdowns. In many communities, schools were closed, and there was general fear about the unknown virus and what it could do to your body. Over three million people died worldwide because of the coronavirus pandemic. Afterwards, many ended up with long COVID, complaining of various symptoms: extreme fatigue, memory problems, persistent dizziness, vertigo, chest pain, and shortness of breath.

For youth, life during the pandemic meant less social interaction with peers. This proved to be brutal. COVID interrupted young people's quests to find themselves, meet someone, begin their careers, and become independent. Though there were major setbacks, it could've been worse without the internet and various social media platforms to keep us all connected. And yet, there was also significant damage from all that online exposure. Many young people bought into the illusion that others were doing better than themselves. Self-doubt crept in and paralyzed them. How could they compete with peers who appeared to be doing so well? And with the rise of AI and fake news, it became harder to get to the truth.

Let's be honest: the social media addiction started before COVID. But the pandemic made it worse. With everyone connected through their devices, we now have fewer face-to-face conversations, less nurture, and, therefore, less comfort in our lives. It doesn't mean we have to accept the status quo. But it does mean we have to work harder to stay connected—physically, socially, and emotionally. Make those phone calls, write those letters, plan those dates, and visit those friends. We have to reach out even when it's hard.

But despite what humans went through during the pandemic, Nature continued to show its beauty to inspire us. And it continues to do so, despite our changing climate and other challenges.

What's Love Got to Do With It?

We all want love. We want to be validated for who we are. But who hasn't heard the expression that *love is blind*? When couples fall in love, they see each other through rose-tinted glasses. Eventually, desire cools down, and differences come to light, usually when important decisions have to be made around spending money, buying a home, raising children, or completing household chores.

Though love can endure, lust does not in the same way—often it blinds you. There are so many decisions to sort through as the bloom of love begins to fade. When you're in love, differences don't seem to matter. You believe love will carry you through the darkest of times. But depending on our personalities and upbringing, we can be triggered. We can go off the rails.

What one person needs, another may reject. Now that gender roles have shifted, it's up to each couple to figure out what works for them. Women now make up more than half of the workforce. To support their working wives, it is no longer unusual for some men to stay home, do household chores, and care for the children, especially when childcare fees are sky-high.

Accommodation vs. Compromise

How do you work things out in a relationship when there is a disagreement? What's comfortable for both of you? I prefer the word *accommodation* to *compromise*. You do things for your partner because you care. *You're not giving in. You're giving to.* Compromise means you're giving up something to please the other, which can be a hard decision for the party who already feels they have too little of a voice. By contrast, accommodating implies giving to your partner out of love. And you hope that they will, in return, give to you.

For example, say a couple is considering going on a camping trip. The wife is not crazy about it, but the husband loves the outdoors. She would accommodate him by making the best of it to make him happy. Similarly, she might ask him to watch a romantic movie with her, which he dislikes. But he says nothing and gives it a chance. He watches it with her because he knows she loves his company and wants to enjoy the experience together. If there isn't any give and take—only take—then something has to give.

In the 1990s, British sociologist Anthony Giddens determined that people who negotiated a relationship that would meet their individual needs were in a "pure" relationship. If, in time, they were no longer able to fulfill their individual needs or asked to compromise too much, they were free to leave. Perhaps this change of perspective is why so many marriages are ending in divorce these days. It's a marked contrast to the origins of a marital union, when you vowed to your one true soulmate to have and to hold from this day forward, for better, for worse, for richer, for poorer, in sickness and in health, to love and to cherish, until parted by death. Though today's wedding vows are similar, divorce is no longer frowned upon like in previous generations. Because of that, some might say it's become too easy to leave. In some ways, perhaps, but leaving a once loving relationship is never easy.

Today, it appears more and more women are rethinking their role in relationships. They've moved on from the time a woman was expected to support her husband's dreams at the expense of her own. Some women who leave their mates today are not complaining about abuse, infidelity, money, or children, but instead complain of being subjugated. Not feeling like their own person. Because Western culture promotes individuality and celebrates those differences, we have high expectations of marriage. People in committed relationships now stress the need to actualize their desires. It would help both parties to have that conversation before they tie the knot.

The relationship was "crushing my spirit," author Lara Bazelon writes in her 2022 book *Ambitious Like a Mother: Why Prioritizing Your Career Is Good for Your Kids*. That sentiment was echoed a year before in Honor Jones's essay in *The Atlantic*, "How I Demolished My Life." She grabs your attention with this statement about the end of her marriage: "How much of my life—I mean the architecture of my life, but also its essence, my soul, my mind—had I built around my husband? Who could I be if I wasn't his wife?" In these stories, there is a sense that the woman's identity—her very sense of self—has been lost because of marriage and motherhood.

In Bazelon's memoir, divorce is viewed as empowering and a source of personal growth—as if marriage is a millstone around the woman's neck, keeping her from actualizing herself. Granted, there are marriages like that. Some marriages keep men down as well, especially when both partners have vastly different interests. One couple met in high school, where he was the school president. Warm and engaging, he loved socializing and feeding his curiosity, but she was a homebody, content to have him to herself. Somehow, they managed to stay together over the years, but he never ceased complaining to family and friends about what he was missing. He looked with envy upon those who travelled and wished he could have done more.

Any relationship takes work and commitment. Fortunately, we live in a time when help is available, even if we are in a rut and can't move forward. We can turn to therapists or counsellors for a fresh pair of eyes to guide us on our path. Friends and family can help if they can offer some objectivity. In days gone by, people were reluctant to talk about their woes; they were too embarrassed to share their challenges. Now, everything is out in the open. We know we are not unique in feeling alone. There are stories galore of people suffering from abuse, mental illness, and addiction. Relationships are not perfect, even for those deeply in love. Accepting imperfection in ourselves and others is not easy. We need to remember we are human.

Maslow Updated

Today, Maslow's Hierarchy of Needs still holds true. A recently updated version shows parenting at the top of the pyramid instead of self-actualization, which is surprising, given that the birth rate is falling in many countries. From the top of the hierarchy, parenting is followed by the need to find and keep a partner (mate retention and mate acquisition), achieve status (esteem), establish social connections (affiliation), feel safe (self-protection), and fulfill basic physiological needs, such as food, shelter, and clothing. We can all agree that these needs are universal. We all need love; we all need connection.

EFFECTIVE COMMUNICATION

I t's unfortunate we don't have courses in school on how to communicate effectively. We cover the basics—reading, writing, and
arithmetic—but don't get the tools we need to get along with one
another.

Learning how to communicate effectively is critical to getting
what we want. We first learn how to communicate in our families
of origin, where we witness how adults behave with one another. If
you grew up in a home where any angry discourse is forbidden—like
mine was—you're shocked when the one you fall in love with raises
his voice, because an open expression of rage is foreign to you. You
might retreat or fight back, not understanding the complexities of
their emotional outburst. Your partner's hostile demeanour may
make you feel unloved. Or if you were raised by a parent who was
a bully, you might grow up bullying others yourself or fall into the
arms of a mate who bullies you, too. Or if you lived in a house full
of secrets, you may learn to keep matters of the heart close to your
chest long after you leave home. Unconsciously, we often bring the
coping skills we learned as children into our adult relationships.

By the time we reach maturity, we've picked up habits that may
not serve us. It all depends on what we've absorbed from our families

and peers. And then there's today's social media-obsessed world, which we have to blame for all rules of decency withering like the leaves on a vine struggling to survive during a drought. Strangers hurl insults, often from behind their screens. The truth is elusive. Staying true to your principles in this fast-changing digital world is challenging for those hooked on social media and their personal devices. It's too easy for some to fall into the trap of ugly communication and say what's on their mind without considering who they might hurt in the process.

TV shows and films are poor substitute teachers. They're a form of entertainment, and though some shows educate, drama feeds on conflict. No one wants to view and hear perfect stories about everyone getting along. It's also not helpful and realistic when disputes are resolved too quickly in television programs that portray conflict. When I was growing up in the 1950s, the TV series *Father Knows Best* depicted a middle-class family with two children—one boy and one girl. It was an idealized version of family life; the parents solved any problems that cropped up, relying on love and logic. I'm sure it left many viewers wishing they had a perfect family like that, which is hard to relate to when your own spends so much time squabbling.

Then, in the 1960s and 1970s, another perfect television family became a staple of American airwaves. *The Brady Bunch* is about a blended family with three sons and three daughters. The Brady Bunch, too, could resolve the problems of sibling rivalry, school troubles and misunderstandings, as if that's possible for everyone.

So, how do we create a family that can achieve such a state or have the ability to find an answer to life's biggest challenges no matter what happens? Well, for starters, we can't because TV is not real life. Back on planet Earth, families are complex and made up of many personalities, so members don't always get along, even when the parents are in sync. When we model our lives after poor communicators in a home laden with conflict, we do not have the benefit of learning how to get our message across in a way that serves us. But with greater knowledge and understanding—which may include therapy—we can improve with age. We all have baggage; it just looks different in every family.

Gaslighting

In some families, communication is so confusing it's disturbing. When what adults say is at odds with what they do, it's devastating to their children.

This family problem was first noted by English anthropologist Gregory Bateson. In 1956, he and his associates proposed that there is a link between schizophrenia—and the double-bind messages that a child receives from the parents. For example, a mother could tell her son, "I love you." But when he goes to hug her, she tightens up. He can feel her resistance and coldness, leaving him confused and wondering if she truly loves him. Bateson and his fellow researchers believed a child is vulnerable to developing schizophrenia if such contradictory messages are given often enough. It's one form of gaslighting.

The term gaslighting, an insidious form of psychological manipulation, was coined from Patrick Hamilton's 1938 play, *Gas Light*.

Made into a movie starring Charles Boyer and Ingrid Bergman in 1944, it tells the story of a wife who slowly goes insane. When her husband—scheming to get her inheritance—dims the gas lights in their home, she notices and comments on it. He tells her it's her imagination. Confused about what to believe, she begins questioning her thoughts and perceptions of what's happening, leading to confusion and a lack of self-confidence. As he continues to question her reality, she grows increasingly mad.

Bateson's work influenced the work of psychotherapists, who were moving away from individual psychotherapy toward family therapy. They invited entire families into therapy to determine how their communication style affected each member.

Besides gaslighting, many other problems can come to light when an entire family is seen by a therapist, who assesses alliances, roles, and unhelpful labels. A therapist can also get a handle on the emotional temperature of the family. Sometimes, they might even be privy to why some family members are no longer on speaking terms.

In psychotherapy, the individual gives their version of the truth, but it's not the whole truth. For example, individuals with personality disorders have skewed perceptions of their relationships, often at odds with reality. It's helpful for a therapist to see them in their partner's presence. Though the practice of family and couple therapy gained traction, it was often difficult for the therapist to schedule appointments with all the relevant family members because of their work hours, unwillingness to cooperate, and other reasons. In these cases, a good therapist can still help the individual. They will read between the lines and guide their patient to better emotional health, whether the family is in the room or not.

Avoiding Conflict

In his book *Choice Theory*, Glasser identifies Seven Deadly Habits: 1) criticizing, 2) blaming, 3) complaining, 4) nagging, 5) threatening, 6) punishing, and 7) bribing or rewarding to control.

Anyone on the receiving end of someone hurling insults, accusations, or criticism feels misunderstood and/or attacked. They often get self-defensive or point the finger of blame back at the other person. And while this is happening, neither side is listening. No one can hear what's being said when voices are raised, expletives are thrown around, body language is threatening, facial expressions are red with rage, and eyes are piercing.

Fighting like this turns into a vicious cycle. The vitriol from both parties only increases with time. The movie *Who's Afraid of Virginia Woolf* comes to mind for its portrayal of a warring couple in an ugly conflict. Elizabeth Taylor and Richard Burton star as the wife and husband who try to best each other. In the end, no one wins. Both parties lose.

The danger of escalating conflict shows up when people dredge up the past and bring up old hurts—what therapists call "the crime sheet." The source of the original conflict gets lost in the barrage of accusations. Everything gets murky.

Glasser suggests we replace the Seven Deadly Habits with Seven Caring Habits to avoid conflict and bring peace to a relationship.

He's referring to the following: 1) supporting, 2) encouraging, 3) listening, 4) accepting, 5) trusting, 6) respecting, and 7) negotiating differences. These habits all contribute to effective communication.

It can do wonders to practice active listening. When we truly listen—to understand, not just respond—we have a much better chance of resolving conflict.

The bumps in the road vary with every couple. How we ride the storms in life can make or break our day. Negotiating differences starts with accepting differences. We often want to share our thoughts and ideas with loved ones. When they don't share our beliefs or think the same way we do, it's difficult to accept . But each human being is unique and entitled to their own opinion.

The Seven Caring Habits that Glasser proposes reminds me of the saying: "You can catch more flies with honey than with vinegar." It means you're more likely to get what you want if you're polite and kind instead of mean and unpleasant.

No matter how we were raised, we've all faced conflict at some point in our lives. Conflict could arise when we are dealing with a rude customer, a domineering boss, an insensitive colleague, a determined toddler, or an abusive mate. The circumstances might not look the same, but we can prevent conflict from escalating by first listening—active listening—which means stepping back and giving full attention to the other party, even if they hurl insults at us or throw their arms in the air. It helps to pause before reacting in kind. By remaining calm, we can respond assertively, but in a non-threatening and compassionate manner. Then, the person attacking or blaming us will be more likely to listen to what we have to say.

But pausing before reacting is easier said than done. Our natural impulse is to attack in kind, assign blame, or defend ourselves. Still, we can diffuse a situation by practicing active listening. And this means listening with an open heart. Mirroring, a form of reflecting what the other is saying, goes a long way toward smoothing troubled waters.

The key to effective communication is using the word "I" instead of "You." It softens any message by telling others what you think and feel rather than blaming them. The following example illustrates how unconstructive it is to use the word "**You.**"

The wife says, "**You** never listen to me. **You** always walk away when I'm talking to you. **You**'re just like your father."

Her statements are loaded. First, she criticizes him and then criticizes his father.

The husband responds, "Why should I bother? Nothing will change. **You** nag and nag. There's only so much I can take!"

We can see how his criticism will raise the emotional temperature in the room. Instead of criticizing, he could mirror her and show her he was listening. He takes a deep breath and responds, "Let's leave my father out of this. This is between you and me. You say I never listen to you."

"No, **you** don't," she replies. *She's still blaming. He needs to stay focused on active listening and not get pulled into trading blame.*

"That must feel awful," he says. "**I**'d be upset, too, if I thought **I** was being ignored." *Again, he's showing her he hears her loud and clear. By using 'I' messages, he's acknowledging how she feels.*

"Yes, it does feel awful," she says. *The emotional temperature in the room is dropping.*

He says, "**I** think **I** yell when **I** don't know how to respond. **I** felt like I was under attack."

"What do you mean?"

Now that he has her attention, he can share his thoughts.

"When you yell, it reminds me of **my** mother. She always yelled at **my** dad. **I** just want to leave when you raise your voice because it reminds me of the fights at home."

Can you see how conflict might end differently with this approach? By stating how you feel using **'I'** statements rather than assigning blame using **'You'** statements, you can do much to reduce conflict. In fact, a disagreement can actually result in greater understanding if you do not resort to blame, accusations, and threats. If you're so worked up it's hard to change gears, it's okay to take a break and leave the scene as long as you make a commitment to return in a short time to resolve the dispute.

You can say something like this: "I'm sorry. I'm too worked up right now to think straight. I'm going to take fifteen minutes to calm down, and then I'll come back and we can talk." Or, if you're on the receiving end of a nasty phone call from someone you love, you might say the following in a calm voice: "This isn't a good time to talk. Let's talk another time. Goodbye." Depending on how they respond, you might even add "I love you" at the end to soften the conversation before hanging up.

Many self-help websites provide other examples of how to communicate effectively in this manner. You're modelling healthy communication when you express your feelings about what has transpired using 'I' messages. This is as true for romantic partners as it is for parents and children.

In his book, *People Skills,* Dr. Robert Bolton suggests using a three-part assertive sentence when trying to get your point across in a conflict. *State the concerning behaviour nonjudgmentally, and the feelings that came up for you and the effect it has on your life.*

In the example above, when the wife accuses her husband of behaving like his father, he could reply. "When you compare my behaviour to my father's—who I know you've had trouble with—I feel demeaned, a lesser man, because I've worked hard to climb out from under his shadow."

To sum up, it's human nature to respond in kind or get self-defensive when we feel attacked. But we have a choice. Rather than perpetuating the cycle of blame, it helps to pause and mirror the other person. It stops the conflict from escalating and helps us get in touch with our feelings. This way, we arrive at a better understanding of what occurred to upset our balance. It also helps us consider what steps to take next.

Effective communication fosters relationships where both parties grow and benefit from each other, much like the living plants in the forest. With sensitive and caring communication, everyone wins. The goal is to leave no one feeling lesser than the other.

We all need positive energy in our lives. Hopefully, we get that from family and friends, a fulfilling career, sports, hobbies, and creative pursuits. However, if the people you love are the ones bringing you down through negativity or criticism, then it's helpful to take a break and get some distance. If you're still emotionally wound up, seek the help of a psychotherapist.

ESTABLISHING A PERSONAL BOUNDARY

A personal boundary is one we set up to protect ourselves from physical and emotional harm. And because everyone is unique, these boundaries differ from one person to the other. Some have rigid ones—they share little and engage rarely with others—while those with relaxed boundaries allow others to interrupt their plans and make demands of their time without a word of complaint.

No matter what personal boundary we establish, we need space to consider our choices, relationships, and dreams. Just as plants need space to grow, we need that breathing room, too. Sometimes, that means stepping back to process a distressing conversation or other form of interaction. This is especially true of any conflict. We may need space and time to evaluate our part in the fight. We may need to determine if what is being requested or expected is reasonable or not. Are we being asked to give more than we can or want to or think is fair?

Letting others crowd us with their unreasonable expectations can only lead to resentment and feelings of powerlessness. When this happens, it's a sign we've stopped thinking about our own needs. We've given into others' demands of us. Feeling hopeless about our situation, we may even resort to passive-aggressive behaviour in our attempt to even the playing field.

A Few Examples

We talked earlier about family scripts and how our upbringing influences our behaviour. For instance, obedient children often become people-pleasers in their adult life. As a result, they're often unaware of when their personal boundaries are being crossed. Not having learned when and how to say "no", they often give in to others' expectations and demands without stopping to consider their own needs. If they think about them, they may put them aside because of feelings of guilt. They've been led to believe they are wrong or selfish to consider their own desires. They've internalized the 'shoulds' that were instilled in them during their childhood and teens. By denying themselves the right to have a personal boundary, resentment can build, allowing depression and feelings of helplessness to set in. Feeling powerless, they may resort to passive-aggressive behaviour to get their way, which further hurts their relationships. But with some self-awareness or help from a therapist, they can learn to be clear and assertive when their personal boundaries are being threatened. They can learn to take a stand and refuse to be controlled; they can make their own decisions.

If you feel inferior or uncomfortable in a relationship, that's a red blinking sign that something is wrong and needs to be dealt with.

Caregiver burnout is another example of losing sight of one's own needs while catering to others. This occurs in families where there is someone requiring extraordinary care. It's loving and commendable, as well as rewarding, to give to those in need, but if you end up sacrificing your own health needs—by losing sleep and a social life for an extended period—you could be at risk of illness yourself. As a psychiatric social worker for the mentally ill and older adults suffering with dementia, my husband dealt with many cases of caregiver burnout. He saw caring spouses and adult children sacrificing their own needs to care for their elderly partners or parents. Love means giving, but if that giving means ignoring your own needs, then you're bound to get sick, if not physically, then emotionally, or both. Caregivers who work around the clock to help a family member may find themselves easily frustrated, quick to anger, and suddenly forgetful.

This is also true for those caring for the very sick or disabled in their families. We may want to ensure they get all the love and care they need, which is wonderful, but at what personal cost? We are human with limitations. Our spirits can break like an elastic when it's stretched beyond its limits.

In the USA, the CDC—the Centers for Disease Control and Prevention—has a wonderful article online titled: "Caregiving for Family and Friends—A Public Health Care Issue." In it, they praise family members for what they do to care for those they love. "Caregiving may include help with one or more activities important for daily living such as bathing and dressing, paying bills, shopping and providing transportation. It also may involve emotional support and help with managing a chronic disease or disability." But when one member becomes so needy and fragile that they need care around the clock, the well-meaning and loving family members may find their own health failing. They lose sleep, become irritable, and eventually burn out. And sometimes, because of the added stress, the caregiver dies before the one they're caring for.

If you are a caregiver who feels run-down, it's worth considering getting outside help. A first step is to recognize the toll caregiving is taking on you. It's saying, "No, I can't keep doing that. It's affecting my health." The next step is to discuss the situation with your family doctor or some other professional in your public health care system. They can hopefully suggest community resources to supplement the care you are giving your loved ones.

Balancing Needs

Considering your own personal needs doesn't mean you're choosing a life of selfishness. Establishing clear personal boundaries means taking care of yourself even when those you care about need help. You can assist and do what you can, but not at the expense of your mental and physical health.

FEEDING

THINKING OUTSIDE THE BOX

We have trouble seeing the big picture when we are too close. We don't see how we can be part of the problem—or solution.

One family drove this point home when they came to me for help with their son who had an eating disorder. The distressed parents had two youngsters: the boy was twelve, the girl was ten. In our sessions, the father sat back and listened while the mother expressed her concern over their son's excessive weight. She stated they both feared their son was on the road to obesity. She also revealed there was a history of diabetes in the family; she was afraid her son could develop this serious disease if nothing was done. While the mother related her concerns, I observed the family's communication pattern. The kids eyed their mother and ignored their father, who gave me the impression he was relatively uninvolved in his children's lives. However, the fact he had come to a family therapy session gave me hope he could play a role in finding a solution. I determined that his involvement was key. I also noticed that, unlike the other family members, he appeared to be managing his weight. Now, he may have been naturally lean, but I wondered if his non-involvement was part of the problem. I decided it was time to shake things up to give the family a new lease on important decisions. I commented on how the father seemed to have mastered staying slim and wondered how he did it. He seemed surprised to have the focus on him but warmed to my suggestion that he help his son become more fit. I emphasized they could spend more time together, and not all of it on diet, but also on other matters that would interest his son. It was a simple suggestion, but one that had escaped the family. They had been so used to the father sitting on the periphery of family problems that they hadn't considered the value of what he could offer.

Our Global Habits

We see Nature in action when roses bloom, tomatoes ripen on the vine, and tree leaves curl under the scorching sun. Everywhere we turn, there are beautiful displays of color. Nature's forests offer us fresh air, a respite from intense heat, and shelter from the rain. Pristine glacier-fed lakes quench our thirst. The earth provides the nutrients we need to support food production. But what are we doing to thank Mother Earth for its bounty?

Our global habits affect our environment. The planet suffers from rising pollution due to increased dependence on fossil fuels. Climate change is on many people's minds. We know we create chaos when we mess with Nature—chaos in our backyards and across the globe. We mess with Nature when we clear-cut forests willy-nilly without replenishing trees. We give credit to forestry giants for tree planting, even though the new saplings can't replace the diverse woods that have been lost. We mess with Nature when we leave behind tailings through irresponsible mining practices that pollute our waters and contaminate our soil, reducing the lifespan of those who live nearby. We do that as well when we practice fracking and challenge the Earth's surface in unnatural ways, triggering a stratospheric number of earthquakes. Through careless use of our resources, we not only deplete our planet Earth of oxygen—a finite resource—and lose forests and other natural habitats to soothe our souls, but we also leave the world's flora and fauna to their own devices. We upset the balance of Nature.

The Earth explodes under pressure, much like we do when faced with too many stressors in a short period. We've had one monster storm after another all over the globe. Ocean warming is accelerating because of rapid climate change. We can expect more extreme weather events to follow.

It's infuriating that the nations responsible for the most pollution ignore the signs of global warming. Unfortunately, oil and gas companies worldwide are more concerned with profits than the health of our planet. It's an uphill battle, but with so many concerned folks toiling away at projects tackling excess carbon emissions, I have hope for planet Earth.

When the world was less populated, we did not hear about how our reliance on fossil fuels affected the atmosphere. When I was a child in the 1940s, my father would heat the house by shoveling coal into the furnace. With no car, we travelled mostly by foot and relied on the streetcar and train for longer distances. Today, both the world's population and dependency on fossil fuels are skyrocketing. We now know these fuels pollute the air we breathe. Our old ways of meeting our energy needs no longer work, not if we want to preserve the health of our planet.

Nature shows us the importance of balance in our environment. She can take a little disruption. Still, when we continue to test her by disrespecting what she offers, Nature suffers, and so does humanity. So far, she's been quite patient with us. But with the increase in weather storms, I imagine she's angry, and I don't blame her. Robin Wall Kimmerer, author of *Braiding Sweetgrass,* put it best. Up to now, "We always seem to be falling and the land is there to catch us."

It behooves us to consider the role we play in the natural world and in our families. For our own sake, we need to find balance not only in Nature but in our lives as well.

PLANTING BEAUTIFUL THOUGHTS

We know how much disturbing thoughts affect us. They can ruin our day and our sleep.

Worrying over matters we can't control is a common human affliction. It's why cognitive behavioural therapy (CBT) has become a helpful form of psychological treatment for those suffering from anxiety. CBT aims to show people how negative and faulty thinking makes them anxious. The main idea is that our thoughts determine our moods. The voice in our head can sometimes be so debilitating that it prevents us from functioning in our daily lives. CBT helps people change the way they think, so it changes how they feel.

Naturally, you would begin your first few sessions with a therapist by unloading your thoughts about what's been troubling you. In follow-up meetings, you would look at what is holding you back from moving forward, understanding that progress is sometimes standing still, even moving backwards before moving forward again. A good therapist will guide you, empathize with your pain, and help you find a way out of the morass you're in.

Finding Support

Those who are addicted to social media can't help but measure themselves against the highlight reels of others living their best life. They think everyone seems to have it all together. Falling into the comparison trap can make them feel inadequate and corrode their self-esteem. This is only heightened if they get involved with peers who take pleasure in bringing them down and undermining their self-worth.

Bullying and abuse happen not only in families but also in friendships. It takes place online with strangers, too. We all need to protect ourselves from toxic behaviour. The first step is planting beautiful thoughts. If we only see faults when we look in the mirror, it will affect how we move through the world. Positive self-talk is critical to our emotional and mental well-being.

The key to planting beautiful thoughts is seeking people who understand us and show us the love we need. It can mean contacting old friends, maintaining positive family ties, or getting involved in the community. We can take part in recreational activities and the arts. We can find joy in volunteer work because it allows us to meet new people and provide a meaningful service to the world. If we are battling an illness or facing another hurdle in life, we can find support groups with people experiencing similar challenges. From Facebook to Meetup to community groups, we can find support if we just look around. We can plant seeds of hope through these connections.

It's no secret that we human beings are pretty amazing. The potential within us is greater than our circumstances. We can achieve more than we ever thought possible as we traverse our unique path in life, following twists and turns and confronting the odd, dangerous curve. We can be like that little plant that holds on and survives no matter what by breaking through cement cracks to showing up on fallen trees. As Leonard Cohen says in his song "Anthem": "There is a crack, a crack in everything. That's how the light gets in."

FINDING BALANCE

All living things need attention. A cactus would perish in the rainforest. A fir tree would dry up in the desert. You can put a healthy plant in good soil, but it won't thrive unless you provide the right living conditions. Gardening is not considered a passive hobby. It takes a lot of work. We fertilize our plants when they're hungry for nutrients. We prune plants to keep them healthy and attractive. And when they multiply or threaten to crowd out other plants, we move or divide them. Much like we would tend to our garden, we need to care for ourselves in ways that support good health.

Maintaining a Healthy Body Through Our Diets

Like our plants, we need good food and a balanced diet. The importance of a healthy diet was underlined in my university years. Prior to getting my Master of Social Work, I graduated from the University of Manitoba with a Bachelor of Science in Home Economics. In that course of instruction, which included food study and nutrition, I was taught Canada's Food Guide, which lists what our bodies need. The guide is not unlike how gardening manuals provide information on the soil and nutrients our plants need for optimal health and growth.

Keeping up with the times and the latest research, Canada's Food Guide has been revised yet again. Today, the guide recommends a diet with vegetables, fruits, whole grains, and proteins that are primarily plant-based. Vegetarians and vegans alike can find useful information to incorporate into their meal planning. The guide also includes caution regarding the amount of sodium, saturated fat, and sugar in our food. Water is also promoted as the drink of choice over beverages with added sugar. The U.S. Department of Agriculture and the U.S. Department of Health and Human Services have their own dietary guidelines online, much like the Canadian one.

But people following a vegetarian or vegan diet need to be mindful of the combinations of food they must consume to ensure they get a complete protein, necessary for bone strength and skin health. For instance, they can combine beans and lentils with whole grains, whether gluten-free or not to get all the amino acids—the building blocks of protein—they need. Those on a regular diet can rely on meat, fish, and poultry for their complete protein and iron needs. Without sufficient iron, a person can become anemic.

Unfortunately, we're living in a time when our foods are not all organically grown, so dietary supplements—such as over-the-counter vitamins and minerals—are needed to supplement our diet. I'm in favour of those, but it's best to consult your doctor or naturopath to determine which ones would benefit you.

Moderation is Key

A balanced diet means eating well and in moderation. So, how do we know when we've had too much? Well, often our stomachs tell us when we've overeaten. We feel uncomfortable, stuffed, and lethargic. Eating late at night can also make us sluggish and reduce the quality of our sleep.

Over-watered and over-fertilized plants show their unhappiness in short order through their foliage and waterlogged roots. Over-watering can be as bad as under-watering. The key to healthy eating is moderation and balance.

If you want to lose weight, Weight Watchers and other programs give examples of good diets. They teach dieters the quantity to eat and the importance of selecting foods from each food group. Through building good eating habits, you can maintain your ideal weight once you've reached your goal.

My father once said, "The best diet is pushing yourself away from the table." We knew this was easier said than done, as we both had trouble managing our weight. My mother's cooking was too good to pass up. And she was one to offer second helpings.

Pushing yourself away from the table might be good advice for some, but terrible for those who fear eating because they don't want to gain weight. Thanks to our media that promotes images of skinny models and celebrities, our society has developed false and distorted notions of beauty. As a result, too many end up with unhealthy body images, believing they are overweight when they are perfectly fine for their body type. If we look back in history, we'll find many examples of artists sculpting and painting a more robust body. I hope we can regain some perspective and celebrate the human body in all its forms.

You can be too thin.

Artificial Food

We need to avoid junk food and other ultra-processed food loaded with preservatives and other additives like colouring. We get nothing in return except fleeting moments of satisfaction.

With the rise of fast food and the number of people in sedentary occupations spending both work and leisure time on their devices, it's not surprising that obesity has increased worldwide. The World Health Organization says that one in eight people is living with obesity today. Genetics may be a contributing factor for some people. If you're concerned, this would be a matter to discuss with your doctor.

We know many physical health problems can befall people who are overweight: heart disease, type 2 diabetes, high blood pressure, certain cancers, stroke, gallbladder disease, fatty liver disease, gout, and sleep apnea. These can be prevented with a good diet.

Dr. Casey Means, author of *Good Energy* and a graduate of Stanford University, laments the fact that medical students get no classes in nutrition. She feels doctors are "missing the forest for the trees" when they diagnose and treat chronic illnesses today. In her book, she discusses how ultra-processed foods, the toxins in our air and the microplastics in our water impact our cellular health. On the

Worldometer's 2024 list of 200 countries with world expectancy rates, United States ranks 48th. An American male can expect to live 77 years. A Japanese man has a life expectancy of 82 years, like the men in Switzerland and Australia. Canada is 20th at 80.5, and the United Kingdom 37th at 79.5.

I'm not advocating for households to banish fast food and junk food, but I believe in the importance of a healthy diet and the benefits of eating well. I'm advocating for people to adopt new habits and curb old ones to keep their bodies working like a well-oiled machine. It could mean indulging in snacks from the health foods section of your local grocery store instead of giving in to junk food. Unless there are specific allergies or health conditions, most people can eat any food in moderation.

It's difficult to say no to our cravings, especially when you've been working around the clock. It's easier to grab a quick bite at a fast-food restaurant and down a bag of chips instead of a nourishing dinner. The problem is that once you start, it's hard to stop. I'm sure this isn't a revelation. We all know this. Many people self-soothe on junk food to help them get through their day. If only it didn't do so much harm. If you fill your body with 'artificial' food—empty calories that do nothing for your body—there's no room for the good stuff that feeds your brain and your bones. Sometimes you wonder if there's a conspiracy between fast-food producers and soda pop makers to keep politicians quiet about the dangers of their products.

Many are blissfully unaware of how our metabolism changes with the consumption of these *pseudo* foods. Study after study shows that our bodies let us down after years of abuse. When we eat the wrong foods, our bodies give up trying to stay healthy. Some people believe we are all vulnerable to addiction, like overeating. Given the amount of junk food that's on display everywhere, that may be true. Manufacturers of food substitutes look for ways to keep us returning for more. There is something in all those products that keeps us hooked. The more you eat, the more you want to consume. However, don't beat yourself up if you slip up here and there. Instead, get back on track by eating a healthy, balanced diet and staying on that path. If you feel full after eating good food, you will be less tempted to satisfy your sweet tooth and late-night cravings.

I had a client who was an obese man addicted to diet soda; he was well over three hundred pounds. He thought drinking the low-calorie drink would help him lose weight. He went through several cases in a very short time. He had come in for marital counselling with his very thin and petite wife. Since he'd had no success losing weight, I was curious about his craving for this sugar-free beverage. Back then, there was little research about what diet drinks do to our bodies and whether they help people lose weight. Though he knew he should eat more sensibly, he was unwilling to wait to get down to a reasonable weight. Desperate, he elected to have stomach surgery. We were supposed to meet again after he recovered. Unfortunately, he died on the operating table during gastric bypass surgery. His heart couldn't take it. Fat is stored not only around the stomach; it builds up everywhere.

We now know that diet soda, combined with carbohydrates, can cause metabolic syndrome—a cluster of medical conditions that increases your risk of heart disease, stroke, and type 2 diabetes. Increased blood pressure, abdominal obesity, and high blood sugar are some of the other symptoms. Diet drinks have no calories, fat, or carbohydrates; therefore, consumers often believe they can eat higher-calorie foods—think French fries and chocolate cake—that they wouldn't have ingested had they gone with regular soda in the first place. This is a false belief. Junk food makes us more vulnerable to serious health issues.

If you are ever in doubt, think about your garden. Would your plants prefer a glass of water or a can of pop? One can might not make much of a difference, but over time, that beverage could cause a lot of damage.

Unless you have some health concerns that suggest you avoid certain foods, there is no reason you can't consume what you want, but again, moderation is key. It also helps to eat balanced meals at regular hours and avoid late-night binge eating. When you eat in the middle of the night, it lowers your metabolism, and you burn fewer calories. The muscles that digest food are revved up and working instead of resting. No wonder people who eat close to bedtime have trouble sleeping.

In 2023, I attended a book event put on by the B.C. Federation of Writers, where I met Rhonda J. Fransoo, the wife of a second cousin, for the first time. She had a table with copies of her wellness and weight loss book, *My Accidental Diet*. It details her efforts to shed forty-five pounds. Rhonda had tried countless diets with limited success; nothing kept the weight off. Interestingly, the word diet now means something completely different to her. It stands for: "**D**elicious, **I**nvigorating, **E**nergizing, and **T**antalizing." What a great twist on a word that is associated with counting calories.

We need to understand our bodies in the same way we need to know what plants can tolerate in our garden. Rhonda discovered that wheat didn't agree with her and adjusted her diet accordingly. Today, we recognize some people are gluten or lactose intolerant. We also know that many others must watch their diet closely for other reasons. Individuals with heartburn, acid reflux, or gastroesophageal reflux disease (GERD) must be careful not to overeat or consume spicy and acidic foods. Thankfully, there are over-the-counter products they can take to deal with the burning feeling in their throats and chests if they want to indulge occasionally. Again, our body will tell us when it's unhappy. It's the best barometer for change. We only need to listen.

Maintaining a Healthy Body Through Physical Fitness

Physiotherapists like to repeat the mantra, *If you don't use it, you lose it.* No matter who you are, there's exercise for all ages and conditions. You will know when you've exerted yourself too much. Problems usually stem from not listening to what our body is telling us.

I was fortunate to grow up in a family that exercised, but not the kind we think of today—their exercise was hard work. When I attended a book club meeting for my novel *Sunflowers Under Fire*—based on my Ukrainian grandmother's life in Russia during WWI and ensuing wars—a reader mentioned that "hard work" is a theme in my book. Like my grandmother, my mother carried that expectation right to the end of her life. In fact, she felt useless in her early nineties when she could no longer make varenyky and borscht, her signature Ukrainian dishes. My family was once farmers in Ukraine and Canada. They worked around the clock seven days a week and only rested during the brutal winter months. But even then, there was always something to do: animals to feed, clothes to mend, handwork to tackle, tools to sharpen, machinery to oil and repair, and pathways to shovel to reach the barn. They were thankful for all the preserves they'd made in the fall; their hard work got them through the winter. With all our labor-saving appliances today, I marvel at their grit and determination to work hard and keep a positive attitude. What saved them was Sunday; on this day of rest back then, all stores were closed, and many people went to church.

The value of physical exercise to keep the body humming was passed down to me. As a young wife and mother faced with my own troubles, I found that jogging for twenty minutes or more gave me an emotional lift. It seemed to take away the problems of my day, much like a hot iron does to wrinkles in cotton. I mentioned earlier that running for twenty minutes activates your beta-endorphins—happy hormones. Gardening, cycling, and walking in the forest also do wonders for my body and mind.

Another Family Example

Though I've been an advocate of exercise for decades, I was frankly surprised by how my husband—who is well in his eighties—recovered from a serious back injury that he sustained during a road trip from Vancouver Island to Winnipeg.

Robert and I had stopped in Canmore, Alberta, for an overnight. He had packed a large plastic crate of dried fruits, nuts, and cereal for breakfast and snacks, but he must've lifted it out of the car trunk the wrong way because he could barely walk after that. I had to not only take over driving but also buy him a cane at the next stop. We somehow got through the three-week trip, but he wasn't any better when we got home. He had to crawl up the staircase of our two-storey home. Feeling that the good years were behind him, he naturally became disheartened. But not so discouraged that he gave up trying to get better.

Robert has always been such an active and disciplined man who doesn't enjoy sitting around all day. It bothered him when he could not exercise, ride his bike, lift weights, and play golf, so he searched for answers. Initially, heavy-duty painkillers helped—the pain was that bad—but they weren't the answer. Not when he'd been warned about the dangers of opiate drugs. Though they helped with the excruciating pain, they were highly addictive. He also tried a physiotherapist, a chiropractor, and a massage therapist, which were recommended by all concerned. They were skilled and well-meaning, but there was little progress.

Unable to do much, he forced himself to listen to his body. In his early years, he had bought the slogan: *No pain, no gain.* But he soon discovered it was a mistake to push his body before it was ready. It only kept him stuck in pain and misery.

But he also knew he had to get his muscles moving again, or else they'd atrophy. First, he had to manage his pain without relying on heavy-duty addictive opiates. He switched to Tylenol. And as a subscriber to The Great Courses online, he found one on pain management called "The Mayo Clinic Guide to Pain Relief," taught by Prof. Barbara K. Bruce, a licensed nurse practitioner with a PhD. It was a godsend. Then he found another program online, offering a gentle exercise called "Better5." There are probably others, but this one is geared to anyone wanting to get going, but gently. The suggested exercises are for the hip, back, shoulders, knees—basically all our joints—and resemble what you'd find in yoga and pilates programs. They're not long—only about fifteen minutes in duration—so they are very manageable. Robert picked what he felt he needed and followed through faithfully. And before long, he was able to give up the painkillers completely. It seemed like a miracle, but a miracle he had played a part in creating by exercising and practicing good pain management. He's now back to his old self.

Robert's story illustrates how our bodies find a way to heal when we listen, pay attention to our aches and pains, and give ourselves a helping hand. There are many stories of people regaining physical movement, even working through emotional distress with a commitment to rest and then exercise.

TAKING STOCK

Forgiveness

I t's impossible to live without making mistakes. The English writer Alexander Pope's famous quote, "To err is human, to forgive divine," speaks to this.

Forgiveness is key to throwing off the shackles of self-blame, self-criticism, and self-loathing. I am referring to the mistakes in judgment we are all guilty of making in our relationships—the wrong word or deed that leaves those we love hurt and confused about our affection for them. When we feel wounded, we carry the pain rather than forgive. We break off relationships with people we love rather than explore what contributed to the negative energy, thought, or deed.

What the Major Religions Teach Us

Forgiveness is core to the teaching of many religious faiths

In the Muslim faith, the Quran mentions forgiveness—at least seven times. Here are a couple: "Those who restrain anger and pardon people; verily Allah loves the doers of good." (Quran 3:134) "Whoever suffers an injury and forgives (the person responsible),

Allah will raise his status to a higher degree and remove one of his sins." (Quran 40:40)

Forgiveness is also a core element of Christianity. In the New Testament of the Bible, Christ asks God, his father, to forgive his enemies: those who've sold him out, captured him, and crucified him. While dying on the cross, he says, "Father, forgive them, for they don't know what they are doing." (Luke 23:34) Christians are taught that they can expect forgiveness if they are truly sorry for their sins because God sacrificed his only son for them. Since the Catholic church believes everyone is born with original sin, the possibility of forgiveness is a comforting thought for the faithful.

Raised in the Ukrainian Orthodox faith, my father, mother, and baba would come to me at Easter and say, "Diana, forgive me for my sins." I would answer, "I forgive you," then ask them for forgiveness of mine. Like confession, which I went to once a year, it felt like a cleansing of the spirit. It was an acknowledgement that I wasn't perfect, that we aren't perfect. But with forgiveness, we can be given a fresh start.

Judaism encourages a similar practice. During the Jewish High Holidays—Rosh Hashanah, Yom Kippur, and the days between—Jews reach out to their families and friends and ask for forgiveness. In turn, they do the same. It's a time to cleanse the soul that harbours grudges over slights or other perceived offenses by others.

Finding Peace of Mind

We humans are a sensitive lot. And yet, some can brush off a slight and not take it personally. They'll interpret someone's hurtful opinion as a comment on the person giving it. They won't give in to spitefulness from someone else. They won't harbour a grudge and seek ways to exact revenge. This is a healthy route to take. They hold on to their power and don't give it to the person who offended them with a thoughtless—or maybe purposeful—remark or deed. They don't react in kind.

Eckhart Tolle says, "Letting go of guilt is a transformative journey that requires us to confront our past and understand the nature of consciousness. By recognizing the distinction between our true selves and the conditioned identities we carry, we can free ourselves from the burdens of guilt and resentment." In other words, we can forgive ourselves.

I am frankly astonished by humankind's capacity to forgive, especially in murder cases. I've read news stories about family members who forgave the murderer who killed their loved one. I don't know if I could, but it must be a liberating moment for those who can do so. Lewis B. Smedes, professor of theology at Fuller Theological Seminary, said, "To forgive is to set a prisoner free and discover that the prisoner was you."

Those who have forgiven have found peace even when their soul remains troubled. They haven't forgotten their loved ones, but they decided to close this chapter of their life so they could move on. They let go of the anger in their heart.

I recall when renowned family therapist Jay Haley talked about this dynamic in a family. When one person throws out a barb, it's like they're threatening you with a dagger. You have a choice to deflect or pull that knife closer. Holding on to the barb affects how you move forward in life. It's difficult to move with joy and purpose when consumed with anger.

The Cost of Grudges

The Oscar-winning biopic *Oppenheimer* gives a good example of a man, so humiliated, he let his anger consume him. The film is based on the life of J. Robert Oppenheimer, the American theoretical physicist who headed the Manhattan Project, which developed the first nuclear weapon during WWII. He is credited as the "father of the atomic bomb," which helped the United States win the war against Japan. Oppenheimer's feud with Lewis Strauss, the Atomic Energy Commission chairman, is an important part of the narrative. Oppenheimer had insulted Strauss in a public place. Strauss gnawed at his humiliation like a dog with a bone. He wouldn't give up until he had done everything he could to bring Oppenheimer down from his lofty perch as a national hero—the most admired man in the United States. Because Oppenheimer had so much public support, Strauss could not get the satisfaction he craved. Instead, he ended up being viewed as a villain by the public and many people in authority. The sweet justice he wanted was nowhere to be found.

When you hold on to an insult or a grievance, you give your power away to the individual who harmed you. To find peace of mind, it's essential to find a way to process negative experiences, especially traumatic ones. For instance, if you can reframe a disparaging remark as an opportunity for growth, you can succeed in reclaiming your power. You can choose to perceive another person's behaviour as ignorant, childish, and unkind—actions that say more about them than it does about you. By thinking this way, you hold onto your power. They no longer have a hold on you. That's the power of forgiveness, an important lesson in religion. Of course, many instances of behaviour are difficult to forgive, such as criminal acts, abuse, and betrayal. No easy resolution there. Still, therapy can help you work through your anger, which could be a mixture of grief, frustration, and helplessness.

Taking a Different Road

W e've been discussing change at length. Does the garden we planted meet our needs? Is what we're doing working? If not, we can change our actions to get closer to what we want.

The Road We Choose

M. Scott Peck's 1978 book *The Road Less Traveled: A New Psychology of Love, Traditional Values and Spiritual Growth* continues to resonate with many today as it speaks to the universal challenge of personal growth. He discusses his own depression and shares stories from his medical practice. He drew inspiration from a poem by Robert Frost for the idea of taking the road less travelled.

On a trip through New England in 2013, Robert and I came upon the *Robert Frost Wayside Trail* in the Green Mountain National Forest by the town of Middlebury, Vermont. It's a beautiful walk through the woods and fields the poet loved—think sugar maples, black and red oak and yellow birch. A board with his poem, "The Road Not Taken," graces the trail.

The Road Not Taken

Two roads diverged in a yellow wood,
And sorry I could not travel both
And be one traveler, long I stood
And looked down one as far as I could
To where it bent in the undergrowth;
Then took the other, as just as fair,
And having perhaps the better claim,
Because it was grassy and wanted wear;
Though as for that the passing there
Had worn them really about the same,
And both that morning equally lay
In leaves no step had trodden black.
Oh, I kept the first for another day!
Yet knowing how way leads on to way,
I doubted if I should ever come back.
I shall be telling this with a sigh
Somewhere ages and ages hence:
Two roads diverged in a wood, and I—
I took the one less traveled by,
And that has made all the difference.
Robert Frost

Frost's poem, "The Road Not Taken," resonates because who amongst us has not thought about the paths in life we did not take.

If we make a tough decision, we can't help but ask ourselves, '*What if I had taken the other road? How would my life be different?*'

Sometimes, one path appears to be better because the other is too hard or unfathomable. Or maybe it's easier to choose the road we think others want us to take rather than the one our spirit yearns for. Or, maybe, as Frost's poem points out, two paths both look roughly the same, and we choose blindly, unsure of the outcome.

Shortly after exploring the Robert Frost Trail, I wrote a blog post to work through a problem I was facing. In 2013, I turned seventy and was on the path to traditional publishing. Though I love to write, I was mindful of my age. I was working on my first novel and belonged to a critique group of writers travelling the same path. The journey ahead looked daunting. It can take months to find the right agent, sometimes more than a year. The process entails searching databases and querying one agent after the other, hoping to find one who likes your work.

I had an agent before for my screenplays and acting roles, so I knew what they could and couldn't do. A literary agent can get you through the traditional doors of publishing, but they, too, can quickly give up on you if there is no interest.

There are countless stories about authors who have had over a hundred rejections before they got a publisher to offer them a book deal. Kathryn Stockett, author of the bestselling novel *The Help* (a successful movie as well), received sixty rejection letters over three and a half years. J. K. Rowling knocked on twelve doors before *Harry Potter* was picked up. It takes time to secure both an agent and a publisher. Even when you have a book deal, you can wait up to two years before your book hits bookstores. Yes, it takes that long for the publisher to come up with a marketing plan, which includes getting the book ready for publication—several rounds of editing, proofreading, formatting, designing the book cover, and setting a date for the book launch. Timing is everything.

In 2012, a well-regarded New York agent showed interest in my debut novel, *A Cry from the Deep*. She thought my story was well written and intriguing, but after hanging on to my manuscript for seven months, she passed on representing me. Though disappointed, I accepted the fact my book wasn't her cup of tea. I could've pitched to other agents, but I didn't want to get into another cycle of waiting for a reply, so I chose a different path. Different roads, same destination.

It's discouraging to get rejections, but I knew I wasn't alone, as most established authors have received many rejections on their writing journey. Stephen King talks fondly of rejection letters piling up when he was young. It's the nature of the business.

I knew I could find an agent, but I was concerned about running out of time. And even if I landed one, it didn't mean they'd be able to find a suitable home for my book. These considerations weighed on me. In the end, I let the clock dictate my path.

Fortunately, I attended the Surrey International Writers' Conference in British Columbia in 2013 and met several authors considering self-publishing. Though it was gaining ground, self-publishing was still frowned upon by major book reviewers and bookstore owners. But determined to put out a quality book, I set out to learn the business of book publishing myself.

The different road I chose was an unnerving one. But I felt encouraged when I learned how many authors had blazed this trail ahead of me: Margaret Atwood (*Double Persephone*), Beatrix Potter (*The Tale of Peter Rabbit*), Jane Austen (*Sense and Sensibility*), Charles Dickens (*A Christmas Carol*), Andy Weir (*The Martian*), Mark Twain (*The Adventures of Huckleberry Finn*), E.L. James (*Fifty Shades of Grey*), Robert Kiyosaki (*Rich Dad Poor Dad*) and Stephen King (*People, Places and Things*). The list is endless.

A Cry from the Deep was self-published in 2014 and received many favourable reviews. Since then, I've gone on to self-publish four more novels. Indie publishing turned out to be rewarding in ways I hadn't expected. Had I not taken that step, I might still be waiting to find a publisher.

How About You?

Are you thinking of pursuing a new direction in your life? Have you been considering other paths out there?

The idea of trying something different can be scary, whether it's moving to a different city or country, making a high-stakes gamble in business, writing about something taboo, or chasing another avenue that feels utterly foreign to you. What if you're wrong? What if you make a mistake?

Fear—of judgment, failure, and the unknown—keeps us locked in the same patterns in life. We can dream all we want, but if we're not feeling fulfilled on our current path, we owe it to ourselves to consider a different road.

What is your inner voice telling you?

Good Stress, Bad Stress

Everyone experiences stress. The World Health Organization defines stress as "a state of worry or mental tension caused by a difficult situation. Stress is a natural human response that prompts us to address challenges and threats in our lives. Everyone experiences stress to some degree. The way we respond to stress, however, makes a difference to our overall well-being."

Sometimes, too much stress can throw us off balance. Managing stress means focusing on what we can control so we don't become overwhelmed by what we can't control.

But not all stress is bad. We also experience good stress, known as eustress, when feeling happy or excited. This kind of stress can stem from going on a first date, winning a game, or enjoying a thrilling ride in an amusement park. Positive stress energizes us. It's the opposite of distress, which is a killer if we don't manage it well.

It's bad stress that keeps us up at night, from worries about making ends meet to finding a job and navigating a toxic relationship, such as a terrible boss. Negative stress can also come from illness, the death of a loved one, divorce or break-up, and extreme weather events. Our busy lives are full of stressors. Now that we're constantly plugged into this hyper-connected world through social media, our lives are literally buzzing with chatter. There is so much pressure to keep up and respond to multiple forms of communication: the ping from our phone, the non-stop flood of emails, the urgent voicemails. It's no wonder we're seeing sky-high rates of depression and anxiety at school and work. If you can't keep up, you feel like you're constantly failing.

The Stress of the Pandemic

During the pandemic, we witnessed an unprecedented rise in anxiety and depression. The world appeared to have lost its grip. Many nations grappled with unexpectedly large numbers of coronavirus cases. Hospitals were overwhelmed; doctors and nurses talked on national television with tears in their eyes about running out of ventilators and beds. Young people were cut off from their peers at a crucial point in their lives, just as they were about to begin the road to adulthood, which involves forming strong alliances with their peers. These connections became impossible when people were afraid to leave their homes. We were told that even those without symptoms could be COVID carriers. Something as simple as going out for essentials became a stressful exercise. There was so much pressure to get vaccinated and protect the most vulnerable population that people who mistrusted medical experts took sides against them and the authorities who insisted on vaccines. Mistrust and fear went hand in hand; there appeared to be no room for healthy questioning. And yet with Nature, we know we can save plants and their neighbours from a devastating disease if we intervene early enough. Unfortunately, we are living in a time when people not only mistrust the news, but also their governments.

The Joy of Stress

While working at Interlock, an employee assistance agency, I visited Teamsters Canada and the regulatory bodies for other professions—such as accounting and law—to deliver stress management workshops. Since I had burned out twice in my social work career, I had taken an interest in managing stress in the workplace. This is a particular problem for those with a Type A personality; they are ambitious, fast-paced, and often impatient for results. They become obsessed with work, always saying yes and taking on more than they can handle. I was certainly guilty of that.

Thankfully, I came across a wonderful book called *The Joy of Stress* by Dr. Peter Hanson around the time when I was trying to figure out how to manage my time at work and at home. From his findings and my own, I discovered the importance of balance. There's nothing wrong with pursuing goals, but it should not be at the expense of a balanced lifestyle. If you are constantly feeling tired, complaining about having no time, struggling to meet deadlines, or sleeping poorly, then it's imperative to step back and look at what you're doing and how you are living your life.

To enjoy life, we need to manage the stress that comes with both work and play. It helps to do some self-reflection. Maybe you're not getting what you need from others because you've been too busy to provide support yourself. How much time do you devote to those you care about? How healthy are your relationships? Are you on solid ground with others? Are you able to communicate with others effectively? If there is friction, take the time to resolve your differences—either meet halfway or agree to disagree. If you have problems and can't manage on your own, seek help. Don't let wounds fester. Like the seventy-three-year-old pensioner I mentioned in the first chapter, don't let that rose prick turn into something irreversible.There are multiple ways we can stress-proof our lives. It's not a perfect science, given that many factors in life are outside our control, but there is much we can do to cushion our journey on a bumpy road.

Dr. Glasser's suggestion for positive change bears repeating: *"If what you're doing isn't getting you what you want, then you need to change what you're doing."*

FINANCIAL SECURITY

Next to health issues, a big life stressor is the worry over financial security: how to pay for the basics and how to pay down debt. When I worked as an EFAP counsellor, on occasion I had people arriving at my office asking for help with their debts. Since this isn't my expertise, I would refer them to a credit counsellor, who would help them manage their debts. With the help of a trained professional, they would come up with a realistic budget, contact the people money was owed to, and agree to some reasonable payments over a set period.

If debt is your problem, it would be worthwhile to itemize every expense and see where you can cut back. Separating the wants from the needs is a good beginning. Keeping track of how much money is coming in monthly will help you set up a realistic budget. A budget keeps us in line. Every company has one. They have the same problems as individuals when they go over their budget and can't find the means to pay off their debts. If you need to consult a specialist, there are many options available. I suggest checking one of the non-profit agencies offering such services.

What I Learned

Given all the problems many people have around finances, it's surprising we aren't taught in school how to create a budget. I was fortunate to take a course on family finance at university, but more importantly, I acquired some basics from my parents, who had learned how to manage their money during a hardscrabble period. They had both grown up poor, weathered the Great Depression, and adopted frugality out of necessity. I'm thankful they passed on the value of hard work and saving money for a rainy day.

How did they do it? They stretched a dollar, like no one I knew. Mom was the original recycler. Nothing was wasted. Not food nor goods that still had some use. They rarely bought items or clothing at full price. Mom always waited for sales. After supper in the evenings, my father would repair some appliance on the kitchen table. Sometimes, the electric kettle or toaster needed attention; other days, it was the iron. He became a self-taught handyman, fixing plumbing and anything electrical. And nothing was bought on credit; my parents saved until they could afford what they wanted. With no car, Dad rode a bicycle across town, and Mom would walk miles to save the twenty-five cents the streetcar or bus cost.

My parents paid rent, too, but they found a way to get ahead financially by renting a house with many rooms they could rent to others. They provided the linens, removed the garbage, and cleaned the bathroom and hallway the roomers shared. On top of all that, Dad worked at a meat-packing plant from 7:30 am to 4:30 pm five days a week, then after supper, joined Mom at the Winnipeg Public

Market on Main Street, where she had been working since 6 am. They managed their produce stall until closing time at 10 p.m. six days a week. Back then, there were no handouts. No food banks. No social assistance. No unemployment insurance. No medicare—the health insurance Canadians get to cover the cost of their physical and mental health services today.

Their roomers lived in small rooms, just big enough for a twin bed and a hot plate. The fridge was in the hall, and all shared the bathroom. They were working women and students. So, though many think the decades after the war were glory days, most still lived modest lives. They had gone through the Great Depression, so anything was better than what they'd endured. They didn't eat out, and specialty coffee shops did not exist. Restaurants were few and far between, only frequented by those who were better off. There were no credit cards to make it easy to buy something. You had to wait until you could afford it. It helped that everyone was in the same boat. If you struggled to get a job and couldn't afford to live where you wanted, you moved and tried elsewhere to make ends meet. Like Dad often said, "Where there's a will, there's a way." His other favourite saying was, "When the going gets tough, the tough gets going."

It wasn't until the late 1960s that credit cards became popular. Suddenly, you could buy what you wanted without waiting until you had saved enough for the item or service. The ability to buy stuff ahead of time became both a blessing and a curse. Many consumers didn't realize then, or now, that if you are even a day late, the interest on what you owe begins to grow at an alarming rate. Credit card companies charge anywhere from 18 to 29 per cent interest, which is compounded daily. Not only do you have to pay back what you owe but also the interest on the original loan (the definition of credit). I think these high interest rates are a crime, but it's how banks make huge profits, something that's not about to change anytime soon. Credit cards should come with a flashing *Buyer Beware* sign. Our busy lives make it easy to miss a payment, so if you're not mindful, you can be buried in debt before long.

Different Expectations

Every generation has its own challenges. Today, many complain about the high cost of living—an issue that can't be ignored, especially in large urban centres like Toronto, Vancouver, New York, and Los Angeles. We have different expenses than previous generations, but we still face the challenge of living within our means. Besides the basic costs of food, shelter, clothing, and transportation, we now pay for our avenues of communication—cell phones and internet services. Add on any streaming services and your bills can be quite high. We also eat out at restaurants and travel more. Back in the old days, it was unheard of to fly anywhere—unless you were wealthy.

Expectations are certainly different today. Not long ago, I watched a television program about housing in Vancouver. The host interviewed four young adults who shared an apartment, which they said they were fine with because they didn't want to work long hours and save for their own housing like their parents and grandparents did. Instead, they wanted to travel and experience what life had to offer.

I recently heard a story about a young man in his early twenties who felt frustrated because he didn't have a house like his grandparents did. When he complained to them, they pointed out his costly habits: consuming weed, taking ski trips, driving a car, and accruing debt because of gambling. They told him he was putting the cart before the horse. They tried to share how they got ahead by watching every penny, but he wasn't interested.

As for students who are university bound, many choose to study far from home. I understand the draw; it's an experience that fosters independence. And sometimes the courses you want are offered elsewhere. Whether you attend a university close to home or afar, the cost of tuition has gone up. But venturing outside your hometown means extra living expenses for accommodation, airfare, and more. Then, there's the gap year—which didn't exist for previous generations—where students are encouraged to take a year off from their studies and explore life beyond their community. If they spend their summers in unpaid work or exploration, then it's unsurprising they're left with major student loans to pay off at the end of their studies. Again, these are all choices.

The choices available today didn't exist when I went to university, at least not for students who came from working-class or middle-class families. I stayed in my hometown of Winnipeg for university and worked summers and weekends to pay for my tuition and textbooks. I also lived at home, which was a huge saving. I didn't know anyone who went away to study. Back then, only the wealthy could afford to send their children away for post-secondary education.

Though young people today have different expectations from those in generations past, some things are the same. Like those who came before them, they crave independence—they want to be masters of their own fate. Depending on their talents and passion, there are many roads to choose from. Those choosing to pursue occupations in health care, technology, finance, and the trades will probably find employment and make enough money to cover rent, food, clothing, and utilities. Some are choosing to supplement their income with side hustles to either make ends meet or save enough for a down payment on a starter home or condo. As for those interested in a career in the arts, nothing much has changed, except it's become even harder to succeed because there are now more writers, actors, filmmakers, musicians, and artists vying to be noticed. When starting out, they have the lowest salaries of all the occupations. Only a small percentage of those who choose the arts as a profession end up making enough to support themselves. They must work at all kinds of odd jobs to pay the rent. Still, their dreams keep them going, year after year, waiting for that big break.

As a writer and former actor, I know the challenges. In my early twenties, I was a member of the Manitoba Writers' Association. I wrote a few newspaper articles and got some attention in an essay contest for a fashion magazine. But with two small children, a mortgage, and a husband who wanted to return to university, I couldn't see how writing would pay the bills. I waited until I retired from my work as a family therapist to pursue my passion. I love writing, but it's difficult making a dent in a marketplace that offers over six million different books. I know many people who are immensely talented and work hard, and yet, financial success eludes them. It eludes them because, besides talent and hard work, they also need luck. It is such a shame that the artists who feed our souls and stimulate our minds with their fine work must struggle so hard. How could we have survived COVID if we didn't have books to read, music to listen to, and films and series to watch? This is not a new problem. There is no simple answer.

These are hard choices, but who wants to interfere with anyone's dream? Where would we be without our dreams?

Wants and Needs

Regardless of your career path and the choices you make, staying solvent is one way to reduce stress in your life. How much must you put aside monthly for the necessities? Once your needs are addressed, you can decide what you can do about your wants. Can you afford to get what you want now? If you can't, what can you do to avoid getting further in debt? These are all important questions to ask yourself. Financial security is a goal worth pursuing.

Garden Enhancement

STRESS-PROOFING

We can take steps to make our gardening easier and more enjoyable with the help of tools and equipment. The same goes for life. There are measures we can take to ease the stress in our lives.

Your Family Relationships

Depending on your family, spending time with them can be satisfying, or it can be stressful. American comedians routinely make fun of Thanksgiving dinner with families. Invariably, there's some relative whose political views clash with your own.

English zoologist and author Desmond Morris views the family as a safe place to be yourself. As the title of his book, *The Human Zoo,* suggests, you can let loose, scream, cry, and laugh boisterously. You can let it all hang out. After all, you've grown up together, sharing food and shelter. Hopefully, you know one another well, both the good and the bad. But Morris also discusses the challenges of living together in a small space.

It's not all roses, but when things are good, love from our families can go a long way toward helping us manage the stress that comes with the various calamities in life. We all need support, but it's a two-way street. You need to invest time and effort in fostering positive connection and understanding with loved ones. Relationships are like anything else in life. If you neglect to put in the hard work, you won't be rewarded with what you want or need from them.

I know there are instances where our effort to provide support isn't always reciprocated. That's why it helps to take an inventory of your support system and determine where you should spend your energy. Some family members and friends may never call or have time to listen, but if you enjoy their company and want to keep those avenues open, then go ahead and make that call yourself. But if you are constantly frustrated with a relationship, you could call them less often and/or pursue others who will respond in kind.

Dealing with Work Stress

Insensitive coworkers and bosses can cause you grief. As an employee assistance counsellor, I heard many instances of people having to take leaves of absence or get medication to deal with anxiety at work.

If your job is causing you stress, take some time to evaluate what it is about the work that's making your stomach hurt and causing you to toss and turn at night. How comfortable do you feel in your role? Do you like what you're doing? Is it the toxic environment that's causing you stress? If you like your line of work, but the people are causing you pain—say your superior is a bully—then it might be time to apply for a similar position in a different environment. But maybe it's the work you find unsatisfaying and stressful. If that's the case, seek the help of an occupational counsellor or a psychologist to help you assess what you're best suited for.

Or perhaps it's the way you approach your work that creates undue stress in your life. I burned out twice as a clinical social worker. I was passionate about my job in a psychiatric ward, but I became over-invested in patients and dreamed about their plights after work hours, trying to figure out how best to help them. When our youngest daughter came home from kindergarten with a picture of her mother surrounded by hospital beds, that was a wake-up call. I loved my work, but I loved my family more. I gave notice at the hospital and found a position at the Child Guidance Clinic, which gave me school hours, a shorter workday, and summers off to be with my children. It turned out to be the perfect position for me.

And yet, as an overachiever, I continued to bring others' problems home with me. I sometimes felt I was working harder on a problem than the client who had come to me for help. Five years later, I took a year off to pursue other occupations, thinking that was the answer. It wasn't. The job wasn't the problem. I was. I needed to find a way to balance my work and home life. I also needed to realize that much was out of my control when working with people. I could offer help, but it was their choice whether to accept and apply it or not.

As I've often said in counselling, life is full of lessons. We keep repeating mistakes until we learn a particular lesson; only then can we move onto the next lesson in life. It took a few tries before I found the balance I needed.

All Work and No Play

The expression, "All work and no play makes Jack a dull boy," first appeared in James Howell's Proverbs in 1659. It means that people who work around the clock without taking a break tend to become bored and boring. Workaholics are obsessed with their jobs. They don't see how their work affects them and those they love. I don't know anyone who has said, "I wish I had worked harder" when they were on their deathbed.

There are many reasons people work long hours. Some have no choice; they need to put food on the table and provide security for their family. Others are climbing the corporate ladder, trying to impress their boss so they can pay for the luxuries in life they think will satisfy them. And then there are those who thrive on their accomplishments. Athletes and artists of every stripe—writers, painters, sculptors, dancers, songwriters, musicians—are known to work around the clock perfecting their craft. The same can be said about entrepreneurs. The creative spark feeds their minds and their souls.

Whatever road you choose, it helps to take stock of your life if you feel out of balance. How many hours do you work per week? How much do you need to work to pay for food, lodging, and the comforts of life? How much pressure do you put on yourself? Or is the pressure coming from someone else? Are people in your family—say elders, children, or a disabled spouse—relying on you? Are they contributing financially? What can they do to ease your burden? If you are working long hours, is it benefiting or harming your mental health? At the end of the day, do you have time for yourself? Do you have time for your family? It's not easy finding a healthy balance between work and play, but working towards one pays big dividends, when it comes to stress management.

Managing Our Emotions

Countless books cite various research on how stress can contribute to illness. In his book *Mind as Healer, Mind as Slayer,* Dr. Kenneth Pelletier discusses the link between stress and four major types of illness: cardiovascular disease, cancer, arthritis, and respiratory disease. In the same vein, Dr. Lawrence LeShan, a psychotherapist who worked with cancer patients for thirty-five years, wrote some helpful books for those struggling with their emotions. His 1994 book, *Cancer As a Turning Point: A Handbook for People with Cancer, Their Families, and Health Professionals*, provides psychological exercises that support patient recovery when combined with medical treatment. We know stress compromises our immune system. When it's under attack, our whole body is weakened. It needs our help to combat stress.

When I worked at the Cancer Care Clinic in Vancouver in 1985 as a clinical social worker in the gynecological ward, I learned about the ravages of this disease and the role stress plays in it. Though I approached my job with some trepidation—worrying about what I could say to people fighting for their lives—I found a lot of hope.

We now know that we all have cancer cells in our bodies, but not everyone's cancer cells get triggered by stress or unhealthy environments. Some of us learn through DNA testing that there is cancer in our family tree, so we are likely vulnerable to this disease. But it doesn't mean we'll get cancer. The information can encouragus to live well and manage stress as best we can.

People diagnosed with cancer feel a range of emotions. When diagnosed with a life-threatening illness, it's natural to feel anxious, frustrated, depressed, and lonely. Some may even feel guilty, like smokers who blame themselves for coming down with lung or other related cancers. These are all normal feelings. We are human. We can't control how we feel. Emotions bubble to the surface without our bidding. But we can counter the ones that get out of control; we can do it on our own or get help.

At the Cancer Clinic where I worked, there was one patient who left a lasting impression. Andrea was a middle-aged woman admitted after being diagnosed with ovarian cancer. She arrived with so much anger, she lashed out at anyone within ear's reach. Granted, she had a right to be upset. Cancer raged through her body. It's a scary diagnosis. Who wouldn't feel like raging at the universe? Even so, she did not have the right to scream at anyone. Fortunately, the staff understood the pain she was going through and did not react in kind, but you can imagine the toll this patient's anger took on her caregivers. Andrea told me her husband had abused her. Years of grievance had piled up for her. Was she like this all the time? I don't know. It was difficult to get her history. But given the role stress plays in our lives, often making us sick, I would guess she had become accustomed to letting out how she was feeling at full throttle, which played havoc with her nervous and immune systems.

There is no shortage of movies and books with a character going apoplectic—with mad body language, bulging eyes, and a crimson-red face—before falling dead from a heart attack. Though these are fictional stories, such characters are often based on what happens in real life.

On the other hand, there's Charlie, a young man diagnosed with a brain tumour. He had a likeable personality and always smiled, but kept his feelings locked up. No one in his family knew how he truly felt. Before being diagnosed with an inoperable brain tumour and given three months to live, Charlie had fallen in love with a divorced woman who had two small children. His mother did everything she could to break up that relationship. As a mama's boy, Charlie knew she could withdraw her love if he argued. His father was no help; he avoided his wife by working long hours. Still living at home, Charlie would sneak out to a telephone booth—there were no cellphones back then—and call his girlfriend. Did these circumstances contribute to him developing cancer? No one can say for sure, but we know bottling up emotions doesn't help. Suppressed emotions must go somewhere.

When his girlfriend came to visit him in the hospital, his mother witnessed how much she meant to her son and finally gave in. She stopped complaining about the woman. Encouraged, Charlie expressed how he felt about his girlfriend to his family. The conflict that had him sneaking out of the house to see or call her vanished as quickly as morning dew in the afternoon. And Charlie recovered, became cancer-free, and lived for many more years.

These are examples of how two cancer patients dealt with their emotions. One raged at the universe; the other withdrew and buried their sadness. Both are extreme. Charlie didn't use his voice; he couldn't assert himself when he needed to. Andrea railed against everyone, so no one heard her lament, fear, and subjugation. It's still a mystery how much emotions affect our health, but we know that stress plays a role. Suppressing our feelings or letting them out full throttle on a regular basis can play havoc with our nervous system, especially if we are vulnerable to certain health conditions.

At the Cancer Care Clinic where I worked, a social worker ran support groups on hope for cancer patients. Hope combats negative emotions and thoughts that pop up when we're sick. A cancer diagnosis isn't a death sentence. Even patients with a terrible prognosis can beat the odds.

A Good Night's Sleep

Everyone knows how awful they feel when they don't get a good night's sleep. As I grew older, I began to suffer from interrupted sleep, which made for restless nights. I no longer got the seven or eight hours I needed. I accepted it as a normal part of aging and didn't stress about my shortened nights. When I talked about it with my female friends at pickleball, they complained about the same problem. I don't know how common sleep disturbance is among women, but I know women spend much of their waking hours worrying about family. And those worries keep them up at night.

The odd restless night was something I could live with, but then I developed insomnia. It was during the time my mother was hospitalized for a pacemaker; while in recovery, she came down with gout and the dreaded C. difficile, which can be a killer for the elderly. She was ninety and not leaving the hospital anytime soon. So my intended week-long stay with her in Winnipeg stretched into two months. I was away from my husband and home, which was halfway across Canada. I was staying in Mom's apartment. When I wasn't there, I was at the hospital. So, it wasn't surprising that I couldn't sleep with so much anxiety on my mind. Unable to function with no sleep, I went to a drop-in medical clinic and was given sleeping pills.

Prescription sleeping pills do not solve the underlying problem. In fact, they often exacerbate it. You can get so acclimatized to the pills that you begin to believe you can't function without them. Furthermore, over-use upsets your biological clock—your circadian rhythm, which regulates your body's physiological processes. In the end, a good night's sleep becomes as elusive as the peace of mind you were craving when you first started taking the pills. If not more so.

With sleep disturbance common among the general population, health professionals have come up with many tricks to help you get the zzzs you need. They can work, but it may mean giving up foods and activities you love. For starters, it's best to develop the following habits to get better sleep: avoid coffee or other caffeinated beverages late in the day, limit screen time before bed, and don't overeat or eat late at night (because your body keeps working to digest food when it should be slowing down). It's also advisable to turn off your cellphone at bedtime, so you won't rush to your device every time it pings.

If worries keep you up in the middle of the night, take them off your mind by writing them down on a notepad by your bed and telling yourself you'll deal with them in the morning. Then think of some positive experiences, from reading an inspiring book to catching a riveting show. A meditation sound recording can also help to distract you from your fears and worries. There are some excellent ones that will guide you through some breathing exercises and put your mind at ease. I have a friend who counts backwards from five hundred when he can't fall asleep. It makes sense because you focus on counting rather than what is keeping you awake.

Some believe having an alcoholic drink before bedtime will do the trick. It might in the short term, but like any drug, it can create more problems in the long run. Experts recommend not drinking three hours before sleep because it will upset your sleep cycle over time. The occasional lapse isn't a problem. Again, moderation is key.

If you wake up late at night, don't fight it. Accept it as normal. Everyone has the odd sleepless night. But thinking you have a sleep problem might make it worse. Your body tenses up because it fears another restless night. It so desperately wants to sleep. Instead of dwelling on the problem, practice positive self-talk to relax. Tell yourself that this is just a phase you'll get through. Don't let that tension take over because it can override positive thoughts. I like to read a book if I wake up at an ungodly hour. I usually have some great novel on the go, so I don't mind reading if I can't sleep—just enough pages to take my mind off what had disturbed my sleep.

There are more remedies you could try. You could drink a cup of camomile tea, eat some nuts, or drink a glass of warm milk with flavouring before bedtime. Both nuts and milk contain tryptophan, which has been found to boost sleep quality. Tell yourself you can do this and come out the other side. I believe in the power of positive thinking. Also, regular hours help. If you sleep at the same time every night, your body learns that this is the time to slow down and rest. It becomes a positive habit.

But also know that if none of the above tips work for whatever reason, then by all means, ask your doctor to refer you to a sleep clinic or specialist. Each person is unique, and one prescription doesn't fit all.

That Sexual Release

Humans are sexual animals. We need the sexual release that comes from having an orgasm. If we don't have a loving partner in life, we can pleasure ourselves. Having an orgasm releases endorphins and other hormones—not to mention a lot of tension—leaving us feeling relaxed and satisfied. It's a feeling that lifts the spirits.

With abstinence gaining in popularity, I assume masturbation is on the rise. It's a natural and normal activity common to humankind and many species for good reason. What could be wrong with an activity that harms no one and brings us pleasure?

Some faiths frown on masturbation or even sex without the goal of procreation. Much has changed in our world. Love for humankind and yourself should be a given. It's up to the individual to decide what's best for them and their conscience.

Lessons from Nature

Nature gets stressed when conditions blunt their growth. When plants are thirsty and undernourished, they can fall victim to all kinds of pestilence. Their leaves shrivel, curl, or get spots, and eventually drop off.

But plants also work hard to deal with stress. For example, the rhododendrons in my garden folded their leaves during a period of extreme cold on Vancouver Island (not the norm for the West Coast). They looked like they were about to perish from the low temperatures. But when the weather got warmer, they opened their leaves again. I realized they had only been protecting themselves from the frost. They were stress-proofing.

I saw another example of stress-proofing in Nature when a deer visited our garden and stayed for days, huddled at the base of our Pieris japonica shrub. I worried she was injured, so I called the wildlife management authorities, who pointed out her behaviour wasn't uncommon. They explained the deer was likely taking a break from dealing with predators in the forest. We can take steps to make our gardening easier and more enjoyable with the help of tools and equipment. The same goes for life. There are measures we can take to ease the stress in our lives. She'd found a calm and safe place in our garden. She was chilling, calming her fears and allowing her body to regroup before returning to the woods.

A Few Words from Voltaire

Voltaire, an eighteenth-century writer and philosopher, recommends taking the kind of break from stress that the deer found in our garden. In his famous novel *Candide*, Voltaire tells the story of three travellers who weather many storms. They have to contend with disease, persecution, war, torture, starvation, and a shipwreck. Near the end of their journey in Turkey, they stumble upon an old Muslim man resting under an orange tree. They ask him about some of his leaders, but he tells them he isn't interested. Instead of engaging in a political discussion, he treats them to a delicious meal with fruits and vegetables from his garden. He tells them to keep their distance from the world to preserve their sanity and well-being and save themselves from the three evils: weariness, vice, and want. The old man's parting words are: *We must cultivate our own garden.*

In his novel, Voltaire suggests that we focus on our own projects, whether it's writing a book, or growing a garden or learning to play an instrument. No matter what we choose to take up, we are better off doing what we can with what we have, and not letting what we can't control occupy our minds and cause us stress.

And yet, there are causes in life that move us. Causes that make it difficult for us to turn our heads away. If you are bent on taking some action that can lead to positive change in your government or country, like fighting climate change, then you need to follow your heart and go where it leads you. However, I encourage you to have balance in your life. Nurture your spirit—make dates with Nature, sleep and eat well, and make time for supportive friends and family. If you feed your soul, you will be rewarded with a clearer mind and a calmer spirit. This need for balance and calm is critical in a world that can overwhelm us with no shortage of tragic news. We need to take a break for our own mental health.

Writing Is Therapeutic

B efore becoming an author, I had a habit of filling up journals, often using writing to purge negative thoughts. Writing can be therapeutic when strong emotions trouble your mind. You can't sleep, think straight, and get on with the joys of life. Sometimes, you can find clarity by writing what's on your mind, as author Julia Cameron suggests in *The Artist's Way*, her self-help book on artistic creative recovery. She encourages readers to find themselves through writing, proposing the concept of Morning Pages, where you write non-stop without censoring your thoughts for several pages. This kind of automatic writing can tap into your unconscious, reveal what's standing in your way, and clarify the direction that will satisfy you. Morning pages can help plant the seeds for change. Many have found their way out of their morass through this simple writing exercise.

Other Ways That Writing Is Therapeutic

—Writing Out Your Pain

When someone assaults you with harsh words or unkind deeds, writing down what happened and how you felt gets it off your mind. It allows you to step back and gain some emotional distance. This *therapeutic writing* is for your eyes alone. By expressing your overwhelming feelings and negative thoughts on the page, you can think more clearly about the steps you need to take to deal with the problem. This is better than hurling them at the person who hurt you and regretting what you said later.

Writing is not a substitute for therapy, but writing down negative thoughts, feelings, and experiences can do much to ease our pain. It's one way to clear mental clutter. Journalling is similar to keeping a diary, except it's filled with entries about feelings and thoughts that occupy your mind.

—Sleeping Better

Getting into bed with troubles on your mind will surely result in a restless night. Keeping a notepad by your bed allows you to write down whatever is troubling you—close to bedtime or even in the middle of the night—so you can address it in the morning. This way, you're taking your mind off your worries, at least for a few hours, while you get some sleep. Sweet dreams!

—Dealing With Unfinished Business

We will all, unfortunately, lose someone we love in our lifetime. It leaves us feeling frustrated and sad because we didn't get the chance to let them know how we felt about them while they were still with us.

When you lose a parent, a child, a spouse, or anyone important to you, writing a letter to the departed is a way to unleash your frustration or pass on your love. It soothes our hearts and softens our hurts when we can write down what we couldn't say while they were still alive.

When my dad passed away, I wasn't there when he died. There was so much I wanted to say. Though I'd lost that opportunity, I decided to write him anyway and apologize. It wasn't the same as being there with him, but it provided some relief. For those of us who believe in an afterlife, there is always hope that what we feel and do can reach the loved ones who've departed.

—Minimizing Conflict with Troublesome People

As we go through life, we are bound to encounter troublesome people—family and others—who don't listen or can't hear what we're saying, or perhaps we're the ones who aren't listening to them. We feel there is nothing we can say that will change the dynamic. It can be infuriating, especially when they are loved ones who bring us joy but also incredible pain with their actions and words.

It's difficult to talk to anyone who is emotionally upset. Rather than confronting them directly, which can lead to escalating arguments and possibly outright rejection, it helps to extricate yourself from the situation and leave the scene as politely as possible. It's also productive to write down what you wanted to say afterwards but knew in your heart you couldn't. You'll get some clarity by writing and reflecting on your thoughts. It might even help you come up with a non-threatening response to still those angry waters. Reflecting on what happened can also help you identify how your response may have contributed to the argument.

Writing allows you to express yourself without inhibition and avoid a confrontation that doesn't serve anyone, least of all yourself. A fight where no one wins can fester like an untended wound. Like the letter to the departed, you can tear it up (or delete it) afterwards.

—Healing Old Wounds

I found writing fiction very therapeutic; it can heal old wounds. There's something about letting out your thoughts and feelings on the page and giving them to your character. Throughout history, authors have woven their concerns into their characters' struggles. It's a common practice. Lorraine Devon Wilke said in one of her Substack articles that writing her novel, *After the Sucker Punch,* was self-therapy. Though the book is fiction, it gave her the opportunity to process some confusing feelings she had about her father.

Say you've had a gruelling experience, and it's still stuck in your mind. You can turn it into a story, a poem, a song, or a painting, and discharge your pain that way. Some of the best songs come from songwriters who've used music to work through their losses in life. They touch our hearts with their musical story, one many can identify with. Today, there are countless songs on Spotify composed and sung by artists who do it for the love of art, and as a way of expressing themselves. Some sing of heartbreak, others of courage, and still others of whatever moves them to put their words to music.

I found writing my second novel, *The Rubber Fence,* cathartic. It was inspired by my work experience in a psychiatric ward—a challenging job that didn't go as I expected. I left after nine months, but my feelings about the system I worked in stayed with me. I got rid of those troubling thoughts by giving them to my protagonist, a psychiatric intern. Though it's fiction, writing the novel served its purpose. I told an intriguing story and simultaneously dealt with the hurt and disappointment that had caused me to change jobs.

—Paving the Way to Better Relationships

All of us have had times when a relationship turned sour. It's just a part of life. Misunderstandings crop up.

Writing can help you prepare what you want to say to improve a relationship, whether it's with someone at home, at work, or elsewhere. Sometimes, what we hope to communicate gets lost in arguments. Perhaps we weren't clear or what we intended to say was never voiced. If you can write your feelings down and then edit them so that you focus on expressing how you feel and what you want without assigning blame, you'll have a greater chance of being heard. Rehearsing those written words and sticking to the script can help you tell a coherent story, especially if it's delivered calmly.

Finding Your Voice

Like gardeners, who find ways to enhance their outdoor space, we can find ways to improve the quality of our lives.

Our granddaughter Chloe Matamoros underlined the importance of doing so in her one-woman show: VOICE: Song and Scream, for the Toronto Fringe Festival in 2023. It epitomized honest, heartfelt, and courageous storytelling. She told the personal story of what she went through at university and how her studies in music almost killed her love of singing. She showed the arduous process of overcoming naysayers, which is especially painful when you experience them in the arts. Stories abound about actors, dancers, and musicians who expose their longings and dreams, only to be torn down by bullies in the field.

Trust yourself is what Chloe sang at the end of her show. It's what she learned through an agonizing process. She felt very much like a butterfly—the theme of her story—one that's emerged from a cocoon because of the pandemic and some disappointing instruction.

Finding your voice is critical no matter what field you choose. We are all sensitive to criticism. Some of it may be well-founded, others not so much. I've encountered many clients who came to me because of their toxic work situations. Since we spend a large part of our waking hours at some form of employment, it makes sense to choose well and take care of ourselves in any work environment.

We all come into the world with unique personalities. Trusting yourself is difficult. We are affected by the people in our circle. For example, I grew up at a time when boys were expected to not cry, but I saw my father cry, so I had no problem with boys crying. Though I don't have a problem, many still do, as the message of 'boys don't cry' continues to be promoted in some segments of society. Unfortunately, that message causes boys and men to suppress their sadness and hide their tears.

I also grew up in a home where my parents rarely raised their voices. Anger was something to quash, yet we know it's a natural human emotion. Letting out frustration is like letting air out of an overfilled tire. It's acceptable to release some of our pain, as long as it doesn't demean or harm the other party.

This subject reminds me of the years I wasted rewriting my first screenplay, *Shrinkproof*, repeatedly. I didn't trust my abilities. I gave way too much power to the strangers who looked at my work and rejected it. Not that it was perfect, but I failed to notice that they also said some lovely things about my writing. Instead, I focused on the fact that they weren't optioning my screenplay. So, with each rejection, I rewrote the sucker until I had squeezed all the juice out of the story.

Thankfully, after years of rejection, I rewrote the screenplay as a novel. I trusted myself to not give up and not take those rejections personally. To quote an old cliché: "Don't throw the baby out with the bathwater." I held onto my baby. I hope you hold onto yours.

We humans have much potential. We are each born with unique talents; it takes work and confidence to put what we've been given to good use. What we all want is understanding and love and the opportunity to exercise our talents. We want to fulfil our dreams.

It seems writer Rudyard Kipling was thinking along these lines when he wrote the poem "If—." In the last stanza, the line, "If neither foes nor loving friends can hurt you," speaks to the need to manage the unwelcome moments in our lives.

If—
If you can keep your head when all about you
Are losing theirs and blaming it on you,
If you can trust yourself when all men doubt you,
But make allowance for their doubting too;
If you can wait and not be tired by waiting,
Or being lied about, don't deal in lies,
Or being hated, don't give way to hating,
And yet don't look too good, nor talk too wise:
If you can dream—and not make dreams your master;
If you can think—and not make thoughts your aim;
If you can meet with Triumph and Disaster
And treat those two impostors just the same;
If you can bear to hear the truth you've spoken
Twisted by knaves to make a trap for fools,
Or watch the things you gave your life to, broken,

And stoop and build 'em up with worn-out tools:
If you can make one heap of all your winnings
And risk it on one turn of pitch-and-toss,
And lose, and start again at your beginnings
And never breathe a word about your loss;
If you can force your heart and nerve and sinew
To serve your turn long after they are gone,
And so hold on when there is nothing in you
Except the Will which says to them: 'Hold on!'
If you can talk with crowds and keep your virtue,
Or walk with Kings—nor lose the common touch,
If neither foes nor loving friends can hurt you,
If all men count with you, but none too much;
If you can fill the unforgiving minute
With sixty seconds' worth of distance run,
Yours is the Earth and everything that's in it,
And—which is more—you'll be a Man, my son!
Rudyard Kipling

Hopefully, we can trust ourselves and make our voices heard.

MIND MATTERS

As we've been discussing, our minds—what we think, feel, and do—play an important role in our life story. Thankfully, we are living at a time when there are many helpful techniques to soothe our minds and help us focus on what we can control, and not worry about what we can't.

Creative Visualization

Creative visualization is a great tool for promoting positive thinking. Apparently, the idea of creative visualization originated in 50 BC, when Cicero, a Roman statesman, promoted the concept of the mind's eye—*mentis oculi*. He described it as the imagined ability to see using the eyes of the mind. And in the fourteenth century, Chaucer wove the same idea into *The Canterbury Tales*. In his story of three men in a castle, one of his characters, a blind man, comes up with visual images.

Author Shakti Gawain takes a similar approach in his best-selling book *Creative Visualization*. He discusses what can be achieved through the art of mental imagery and affirmation. If you can think of yourself in a positive light and visualize yourself that way, then you can fulfill your aspirations. In one of his examples, Gawain suggests you can use visualization to improve a relationship gone sour. First, you meditate, and then, in that quiet state, you imagine yourself and the other person communicating in an open, honest, and pleasant manner.

Sports psychologists encourage the athletes they work with to use this technique in their practice and play. Though this idea has been around for centuries, it's one that continues to pay dividends when applied by those who want to actualize their dreams and are willing to put work into improving their skills.

Meditation and Mindfulness

Neurologists have found that we use only a small portion of our brains. We have so much potential. We have the ability to figure things out when the going gets rough, but we have to get out of our own way. Meditation and Mindfulness are practices that help us to do just that.

Meditation is the act of paying attention to only one thing. It's a way to become calm, find clarity, and improve awareness. By doing so, you put aside your rambling thoughts. If they're troublesome, you'll hopefully conclude that your thoughts are not facts. When your mind dances around, jumping from one frustrating thought to the next without focus, it can add to the distress you might be feeling. Meditating gives you the opportunity to slow down. You start by focusing on your breath to calm your troubled waters. It's not unlike leaving six lanes of traffic in Los Angeles and finding that Zen Garden with a pond, a little babbling brook, or a waterfall, where you can empty your mind and let it rest.

There are many types of meditation. One is *mindfulness*, which is achieved by focusing on the present moment and accepting one's feelings, thoughts, and bodily sensations. Jon Kabat-Zinn, a professor of medicine emeritus at the University of Massachusetts Medical School, pioneered the meditation movement in the United States. He is known for creating the Mindfulness-Based Stress Reduction Clinic and the Center for Mindfulness in Medicine, Health Care, and Society at UMass. His books became bestsellers when he was featured in Bill Moyers' documentary series *Healing and the Mind*.

Kabat-Zinn has voiced several audio tapes, guiding the listener through mindfulness exercises. Through practice and over time, you can shut out the world and give your mind a rest, even if only for a little while. You're being present by focusing on breathing in and out to clear the mind.

When we're consumed with negative thoughts that fuel our anger or keep us anxious, it's easy to feel like a victim. We ruminate on the times we felt misunderstood, maligned, or disrespected. We all have those dark thoughts. We encounter problems when we don't acknowledge our negative thoughts or give space to them. Accepting them and understanding they are just thoughts, we can begin to choose what we want to focus on in our lives. By practicing mindfulness, we are making room for what will nourish our mind and soul. We're accepting what is.

Eckhart Tolle, a spiritual teacher, wrote *The Power of Now: A Guide to Spiritual Enlightenment* after he recovered from a debilitating depression. He found some peace during an early morning walk on London's streets. He marvelled at that sense of peace and explored how to cultivate that feeling. In his book, he encourages readers to shift their thinking by concentrating on the present. By doing so, they awaken a deeper understanding of themselves.

Thich Nhat Hanh, a Vietnamese peace activist and Buddhist monk, often considered "the father of mindfulness," left us with many memorable quotes before passing away in 2022 at the age of ninety-six. In tune with Nature, he had a lot to say about empathy. This quote is worth noting: "When you plant lettuce, if it does not grow well, you don't blame the lettuce. You look for reasons it is not doing well. It may need fertilizer, more water, or less sun. You never blame the lettuce. Yet if we have problems with our friends or family, we blame the other person. But if we know how to take care of them, they will grow well, like the lettuce. Blaming has no positive effect at all, nor does trying to persuade using reason and argument. That is my experience. No blame, no reasoning, no argument, just understanding. If you understand, and you show you understand, you can love, and the situation will change."

There's a lot to unpack with this quote. Love and understanding can take you far in your relationships. Looking to ourselves for the answer is key. Diverting attention from yourself and blaming others for your predicament keeps you from growing and taking responsibility for your choices. Blame goes nowhere; it only builds resentment.

"Nothing ever goes away until it teaches us what we need to know," said Pema Chodron, an American-born Tibetan Buddhist teacher. Life is a series of lessons. There is no one course of study that fits all. Each journey is individual. It helps to treat our own with kindness, and not compare it to others.

The Fruits of Your Labour

THE GARDENER IN YOU

With your garden planted, you can sit back and enjoy the fruits of your labour—cut some flowers to grace your dining table, pick some vegetables to roast for dinner, and watch butterflies and bees flit from bloom to bloom, ensuring that Nature carries on.

Though your emotional regulation skills may improve, you still have to weed from time to time, so that what you want to grow and enjoy continues to flourish. Life, like Nature, might unleash its fury in unexpected moments, testing your fortitude.

Because we don't know what storms lie ahead, here are a few more thoughts on how to keep our life's gardens vibrant and healthy.

As discussed earlier, there is much we can do on our own if we put our minds to it. The weight of our emotions keeps us from resolving our problems. If we're depressed, it's hard to move forward. If we've been wronged somehow, our anger and frustration can get the best of us. Keeping fit with regular exercise and a healthy diet goes a long way toward keeping our spirits up. But if you haven't developed these good habits, you can easily feel overwhelmed when your life gets out of control.

It's not unlike conquering a mountain. A mountain climber could look at a peak thousands of feet above sea level and say, "Hell no, I'm not climbing that." But that's not what they do. They prepare well for all the inevitable ways their ascent might be interrupted; they psych themselves up and say they can do it, then take off and handle that summit—one footstep at a time. It's similar to what A.A. advocates say in their twelve-step program; they promote the idea of moving forward, one step at a time.

We don't have to solve everything that troubles us at once. With perseverance and our goals in mind, it's incredible what we can accomplish.

What Our Dreams Tell Us

Have you ever woken up questioning the meaning of your dreams? Whether they are pleasant, confusing, or nightmarish, dreams are an untapped resource for figuring out what's going on in our emotional garden.

In my therapy practice, I would occasionally do some dream analysis. I come by it honestly. I grew up with a mother and a grandmother who sat at the kitchen table every morning to discuss their dreams. Their interpretations were based on old folklore. For instance, if you were laughing in your dream, it meant you would be crying soon and vice versa.

Though my family's understanding of dreams had been passed down for generations, my approach to interpreting dreams is based more on Gestalt therapy. The idea is that every part of our dream is some aspect of ourselves. If we take the time to reflect on what we dreamed, we can often find a connection. We'll find that even when we're asleep, our minds are busy trying to solve our problems.

In my childhood and early adulthood, I used to have a recurring dream about a man coming up the staircase to my bedroom. I could only see his shadow looming large on the wall above the steps. He moved slowly, the stairs creaking ominously with each footstep. As he got closer, I was a victim in waiting, paralyzed with fear, unable to scream for help. I'd wake up just before the bad guy got to my door. When I got older, I realized I had internalized some of the scary scenes in the film noir movies I'd seen as a child. My mother loved movies, and we went weekly to see a double feature at a cinema on Main Street in Winnipeg. Back then, film noir was popular. Shot in black and white, the films showed villains creeping up the stairs, casting long dark shadows on the white walls of the staircase, getting closer to their target's room.

My bad dreams stopped in my twenties when I took up karate. Because I had taken some martial arts classes, I suddenly felt stronger, more capable, and able to handle any stranger who had thoughts of hurting me in any way. I was now psychologically prepared to take on any assailant in my bad dreams. What I learned was powerful. I could change the outcome with the power of my mind. The fear in my bad dream was a comment on my personality as well. I've never been a courageous person, but I discovered I had more power than I thought and how to exercise it.

Before going to bed, we can tell ourselves we can change the ending if we have a recurring nightmare. We can decide what ending we'd prefer and plant that in our mind. When we get to the threatening part of our dream, we can wake ourselves up or prevent the bad thing from happening. We can suggest an alternate ending. The power of our thoughts can change the outcome.

One of my clients had a recurring nightmare about a spider crawling over her at night. She wished she had something to get at it. To swat it, I suggested she put a slipper under her bed before she went to sleep. She returned weeks later, telling me it had worked. The bad dream had stopped. She never had to use the slipper. But just having it there gave her the feeling she had some control. It was the power of her mind. By taking action rather than giving in to helplessness, she was able to take charge and stop the nightmare from recurring.

Often, what we dream about is what's most pressing to us. By writing it down, we bring our unconscious to the surface. We can begin to see how these unlikely scenes in our dreams are connected to the problems we're trying to solve. I love that about dreams; it's another resource in life's toolbox.

LESSONS FROM A LONG-DISTANCE SWIMMER

The film *Nyad,* starring Annette Bening and Jodie Foster, tells the story of long-distance swimmer Diana Nyad, who swam from Cuba to Florida when she was sixty-four. So many had tried before her, and they were much younger. How did she accomplish this impossible feat?

She had tried at twenty-eight and failed. When she reached sixty, she tried again. There were so many naysayers, but she refused to abandon her dream. She pulled a team together and set out on her swim. She had prepared mentally and physically for the long-distance swim, but in the end, the elements proved too strong for her to overcome. There were sharks and jellyfish in the water. Notably, the box jellyfish can easily kill a swimmer once they make contact. She not only had to contend with these sea creatures, but she also had to be mindful of currents that could pull her off course, forcing her to swim more miles than she intended. Yet, she persevered under these dangerous conditions, which included storms with wicked waves and thunder. Though she had prepared physically, it turned out to be too much. She failed three more times.

Her supporters suggested she quit. But she refused to give up. Again, she assembled a team to ensure she would be rescued if there was any danger. They would also feed and hydrate her and provide medicine if she became sick. All this had to be done without touching her. Undaunted and now sixty-four, she set out for a fifth time. Days later, she stumbled onto the shores of Florida, so happy. She had realized her dream; she had succeeded.

We don't have to pursue lofty goals like Nyad's. The ones we choose should fit our needs and personality. I've seen people give up before they even start working towards the simplest goal: completing a course, studying for an exam, applying for a job, taking up a new hobby, or joining a community group. They look at each task as if it is a mountain. If we look at life like a ladder leading us to better things, why wouldn't we climb it—one rung at a time?

Nyad's achievement didn't happen overnight. It took hard work, practice, and courage. She also believed in herself and didn't give up, even when those around her encouraged her to quit.

Though we applaud Nyad's accomplishment, we also need to applaud those who recognize their limits and are content to go no further. It's a sign of health to know what's possible. Success can be as simple as living life well, with no heroics or fanfare.

Idleness Redefined

Idleness has always been frowned upon. The origins of the proverb, "Idle hands are the devil's playground," are unknown but repeated from one generation to the next, warning others about the sin of doing nothing. Benjamin Franklin said, "It is the idle man who is the miserable man." I'm sure he wasn't referring to those moments when he stared into space, thinking about his work and how he could make light from electricity. This was idle time, but while he was doing nothing, his brain kept going, imagining all kinds of possibilities. Idle time is often when we are the most creative. During these quiet moments, we have an opportunity for reflection and the time to solve the puzzles of our day.

If you're on any social media platform, it doesn't take long to absorb the message that others lead very productive and interesting lives. Though this illusion affects the young more—the competition for attention is fierce—it also affects the older generation. Technology, which was supposed to save us precious hours, is actually stealing our time and attention. We feel we need to always be available. Our cellphone pings constantly, notifying us of updates about family, friends, or world news. We feel the need to read every notification and respond, or else we feel disconnected. Keeping up with this demand is taxing, especially for the younger generation trying to find their way. Some parents unknowingly reinforce this expectation when they complain that their children—young or adult—don't respond in a timely manner to a voice message, text, or email. And many employers also expect their employees to be at their beck and call.

Life in the fast lane has been a common way to live for decades. At least it was until the pandemic hit in March 2020. Suddenly, with news of the virus spreading, offices and other workplaces emptied, and people hunkered down in their homes. This worldwide lockdown continued for two years before people came out of hiding. In late 2024, we were still coming down with the illness, but the public no longer had the same fear. Most of the world's population is vaccinated. We also know we can safely venture outside if we wear masks and wash our hands frequently.

The fear and isolation of the pandemic gave people time to think. They could ponder about their options in life. This is what doing nothing does for you. It gives you time. It allows the creative juices to flow once more.

Henry Ford, the business magnate who popularized the auto assembly line, understood that idle time was needed for creativity. He was giving a tour of his plant one day when a visitor commented on a man sitting at an empty desk with his feet up. He appeared to be doing nothing. Ford said, "A few years ago, that man came up with something that saved me $2,000,000. And when he had that idea, his feet were exactly where they are now." He added, "Thinking is the hardest work there is, which is probably the reason so few engage in it."

Just Being Is Enough

In recent times, the concept of staying idle for the sake of slowing down has gained ground. The Danes and Norwegians call it "hygge," which means taking time away from the busyness of life to enjoy quiet pleasures. Cozying up with family for a movie night. Enjoying a candle-lit bubble bath. Knitting or reading by the fireplace. Catching up with friends over a hearty meal. Warmth and laughter. These comforts in life all fall under the definition of "hygge."

The Swedes have also embraced a mindset based on moderation and sustainability, which they call "lagom"—the word for "just the right amount." They believe in a balanced life, which is a way to tackle the stress of trying to do too much with too little time.

And like their Scandinavian neighbours across the water, the Dutch believe in the concept of "doing nothing," which they call "niksen." It might look like idleness to a busy person, but it's actually a way to manage stress. This Dutch wellness trend is all about simply being instead of being present, perhaps just listening to music or enjoying anything without purpose. This is how niksen differs from mindfulness. With the latter, you're present in the moment; with the former, you're allowing your mind to wander. It could be the simple act of sitting, staring out the window, or lying on the grass contemplating the clouds above. Engaging in niksen can lead to many *aha* moments, like the one Ford mentioned when he gave a tour of his factory.

In her book, *Deviced!: Balancing Life and Technology in a Digital World,* psychologist Doreen Dodgen-Magee compares niksen to a car whose engine is running but not going anywhere Taking a break from our daily go-go-go lives is not unlike taking that breath of fresh air when the sky clears after a thunderstorm. It's that moment when you take it all in: the wet pavement, the drops of water on tree leaves, the sound of splashing puddles as cars drive by, the footsteps of people hurrying home with an umbrella in one hand and a bag of groceries in the other. And when you allow your mind to wander, there are no barriers to where it can go. Creativity comes from a clear mind. We need time to find clarity and come up with new ideas. But again, there is no prescribed way of being because each person is unique. A prescription would be self-defeating. When you practice niksen, you're giving yourself permission and freedom to do nothing for a little while.

But you might wonder about rent and all the bills to pay. Practicing niksen doesn't mean sloughing off responsibilities or quitting your job. It means finding time in your busy life to do nothing without feeling guilty.

Putting away your devices is a start. More and more people are putting them in silent mode, letting whatever is happening on social media and around the world go by. It'll still be there when you decide to tune in again.

It's all about balance.

A Closing Thought

In our busy world today, we sometimes lose sight of the need to be still, observe, and just be. Even Nature takes a break. Plants thrive in the glorious summer months, only to wither and die in the fall. But many don't perish. They just rest and hibernate. They carve out time to sleep, regroup, and prepare for another surge of life in the spring.

My ancestors were farmers. They worked non-stop throughout spring, summer, and fall. And like Nature, they took a break in the winter months. Though they continued to care for their livestock and used the slower time to prepare for the coming year, it was also a time of relaxation.

During the latter years of my private practice, I became more of a guide than a therapist. In a way, what I did could be compared to what a forest guide does by pointing out plants to note, paths to take, and things to be aware of for safety and well-being. A guide doesn't walk for those following them on the path. They trust that with some information, the hikers can manage just fine. Similarly, I helped clients see what they couldn't see and gave them empathy while they figured things out. People are generally more than capable of finding their own way in an atmosphere filled with love and understanding.

No life is perfect. It's the human condition. We all have challenges. Unfortunately, some face more adversity than others. The trick is to tackle problems before they accumulate and wear you down. It takes strength, courage, and willingness to look at ourselves, one step at a time.

I'm thankful for all those who trusted me with their stories. I value these individuals, their lives, and their families. I learned much from them, as I hope they did from me.

Acknowledgements

This book has been percolating for decades. I have many people to thank for their stories and support—my fellow workers (social workers, psychologists, psychiatrists, psychiatric nurses), clients, and teachers.

My parents, Peter and Dolly Klewchuk, who are now long gone, showed me a model of a life well-lived. Remembrance of their love and laughter still carries me through good and bad times. I am grateful for my baba, Lukia Mazurec, who was a pillar of faith, strength, and wisdom. She taught me that the most important thing in life is family.

Author Jocelyn Reekie, a wonderful friend, generously contributed to this book by sharing her husband's treatment for Alzheimer's in the section called *The Problem with Labels*. Her thoughts underline one of the challenges we all face when we are vulnerable and unable to have our voices heard in the healthcare system. No one knows the pain someone else goes through, yet we are richer for it when someone shares their story. We learn and grow in our understanding of the human condition. Though there is much we can control, there's much we can't. That's when we rely on the love and empathy of others.

I am grateful that my daughters Karen and Robyn, friends Sue Cohene, Judy Johns, Rose Marie DePaoli, and Rod Baker read my work before publication. I appreciate their time and valuable feedback. And a special thanks to granddaughter Chloe for sharing her story.

My editor, Jennifer Cheng, went through my manuscript with a fine-tooth comb. I'm thankful for her suggestions and comments.

I wrote this book with the loving support of my husband, Robert, who was my first reader. He's always at my side, encouraging me. He is my rock.

Bibliography

Bank, Dylan, Samara Abramson, and Mark Abadi. "How a Pioneering Brain Surgery Helped a Man Who'd Been Addicted to Opioids for 18 years Find Sobriety." *Business Insider.* Sept. 15, 2020.

Barry, Susan R. PhD. "How to Grow New Neurons in Your Brain." *Psychology Today.* Jan. 16, 2011.

Bazelon, Lara. *Ambitious Like a Mother: Why Prioritizing Your Career is Good For Your Kids* Little, Brown Spark, 2022.

Bolles, Richard M. *What Color Is Your Parachute?* Ten Speed Press; Revised edition 2022.

Bolton, Robert, Ph.D. *People Skills: How to Assert Yourself, Listen to Others, and Resolve Conflicts.* Touchstone, 1986.

Breggin, Peter R. M.D. *Toxic Psychiatry.* St. Martin's Press 1991.

Davidson, Jordan. "8 Things That Happen When You Finally Stop Drinking Diet Soda." Womenshealthmag.com June 8, 2015.

Davis, B. & K. Francis. "Mind's Eye (Mentis Oculi)" in Discourses on Learning in Education. 2023. Found on www.learningdiscourses.com website.

Eliot, T.S. *A Choice of Kipling's Verse.* Faber & Faber, 1943.

Fitzgerald, Sunny. "The secret to mindful travel? A walk in the woods." *National Geographic.* Oct. 18, 2019.

Glasser, William M.D. *Reality Therapy: A New Approach to Psychiatry* Harper Perennial 1975.

Glasser, William M.D. *Counseling with Choice Theory: The New Reality Therapy* Harper Perennial 2001.

Gómez José M., A. Gónzalez-Megías, A., & M. Verdú. The evolution of same-sex sexual behaviour in mammals, published online in *nature communications* by Oct. 03, 2023.

Gray, John. *Men Are from Mars, Women Are from Venus.* Harper Paperbacks 2016.

Haley, Jay. *Problem-Solving Therapy.* Jossey-Bass; 2nd edition 1987.

Hamilton, Kristy. *Nature's Wild Ideas* Greystone Books, 2022.

Jones, Honor. "How I Demolished My Life." *The Atlantic,* Dec. 31, 2021.

Kolata, Gina. "An Ultrasound Experiment Tackles a Giant Problem in Brain Medicine." *New York Times* Jan. 14, 2024.

Lefley, Harriet P. PhD. "Temperament: Theory and Practice." *TheAmerican Journal of Psychiatry,* Vol. 155, Number 1, Jan. 1, 1998.

Maslow, A. H. "A theory of human motivation." *Psychological-Review, 50* (4), 370-96. 1943.

Means, Casey M.D. withMeans, Calley. *Good Energy.* Avery, 2024.

O'Neill, Nena and George O'Neill. *Open Marriage:A New Lifestyle for Couples.* M. Evans & Company; Revised edition 1984.

Peck, M. Scott. *TheRoad Less Traveled: A New Psychology of Love, Traditional Values, andSpiritual Growth* Touchstone Press, 1978.

Piccoli, Rob. *BlessedAre the Contrarians: Diary of a Journey Through Interesting Times*. CreateSpace Independent Publishing Platform, 2012.

Pope, Alexander and Rogers,Pat. *The Major Works (Oxford World's Classics)*. Oxford University Press;Reissue Edition (March 15, 2009).

Polderman, Tinca J C;Benyamin, Beben; de Leeuw, Christiaan A; Sullivan, Patrick F; van Bochoven,Arjen; Visscher, Peter M; Posthuma, Danielle (2015). "Meta-analysis of theheritability of human traits based on fifty years of twin studies." *Nature Genetics*. 47.

Rifkin, Mark. *When Did IndiansBecome Straight?: Kinship, the History of Sexuality, and Native Sovereignty*.Oxford: Oxford University Press, 2011.

Rodriguez, Tori. "Descendantsof Holocaust Survivors Have Altered Stress Hormones." *Scientific American*. March1, 2015.

Satir, Virginia *Conjoint Family Therapy*. Science and Behaviour Books 1983.

Smithers, Gregory D. *ReclaimingTwo-Spirits: Sexuality, Spiritual Renewal, and Sovereignty in Native America*. Boston:Beacon Press, 2022.

University of Cambridge."Brain Charts Map the Rapid Growth and Slow Decline of the Human Brain Over OurLifetime." *Neuro sciencenews.com* April 6, 2022.

Van Der Kolk, Bessel. *TheBody Keeps the Score: Mind, Brain and Body in the Transformation of Trauma*. PenguinBooks Ltd, 17th ed. 2015.

WallKimmerer, Robin. *Braiding Sweetgrass: Indigenous Wisdom, ScientificKnowledge, and the Teachings of Plants.* Milkweed Editions, 2015.

Wasik, Barbara and Donna Bryant. "Home Visits and FamilyEngagement" by Barbara Wasik and Donna Bryant, *Encyclopedia of Social Work*.March 22, 2023.

Wohlleben, Peter and Tim Flannery et al. *The Hidden Lifeof Trees: What They Feel, How They Communicate—Discoveries from A Secret World*.Greystone Books, 2016.

Wolynn, Mark. *It Didn't Start With You: HowInherited Family Trauma Shapes Who We Are and How to End the Cycle.* PenguinLife, 2017.

About the Author

Diana Stevan is the author of the award-winning novel *Sunflowers Under Fire* and its sequels *Lilacs in the Dust Bowl* and *Paper Roses on Stony Mountain*. It's a historical fiction series based on her grandmother's life in Ukraine. Before writing the trilogy, Diana wrote the time-slip romantic mystery *A Cry from the Deep* and the psychological novel *The Rubber Fence*.

She's had poetry published in the international arts journal *Dream Catcher* and a short story in the anthology *Escape*. She has also penned magazine and newspaper articles.

Her varied background includes work as a clinical social worker, a family therapist, a teacher, an actress, a model, and a CBC television sports broadcaster. Diana lives with her husband, Robert, on Vancouver Island and in West Vancouver, British Columbia.

For more, visit her website: https://www.dianastevan.com